AF264381

Blessed by God

Blessed by God

David Beresford

Brookscraft Publishing

Blessed by God

Published 2026 by:
Brookscraft Publishing
Buffalo, New York 14203
info@brookscraftpublishing
https://brookscraftpublishing.com

First published in 2025 by Cedar Tree Books.

ISBN: 978-1-969682-30-8 EBOOK
ISBN: 978-1-969682-31-5 PAPERBACK
ISBN: 978-1-969682-32-2 HARDCOVER

Title : Blessed by God
Author: David Beresford
Editor: Nicholas L. Cerchio, III
Book Design: Bob Schwartz
Cover image : Chursina Viktoriia/shutterstock.com
Copyright: © 2025 David Beresford

To Sherri Howell

who is blessed by God and who loves the Lord

But you too, who have heard and have believed, are blessed.

Every soul who has believed both conceives

and generates the Word of God and recognizes his works.

Saint Ambrose

Bishop of Milan
A.D. 339-397

Table of Contents

Foreword

In his latest book, *Blessed By God*, David Beresford takes themes that we can all relate to—like *home*, *politics*, and *peace*—and weaves throughout them profound reflections for each of us to ponder and pray over. Beresford provides us with a very accessible way to pray through our daily circumstances, which sometimes involve episodes of struggle, peace, and even questioning. I especially appreciate Beresford's reflections on questions like, "Where is Home?" as in this example about rock musician Duane Allman:

> *At the time the band was continually touring. Asked if he ever got the chance to live at home, Allman replied, 'Gypsies ain't got no home, I'm at home when I'm with my people; I'm always at home, I'm home now.'*

In these times of political division and strife, Beresford dares to attend to the topic of politics and how we as Christians need to approach this difficult subject prayerfully:

> *Sometimes, churches take sides. This is a mistake, I believe, and often results in a hijacking of the gospel to feed a political vanity. Because I want the Church of the Messiah to be a spiritual home for Democrats and Republicans alike, I will avoid the temptation to speak out or advocate for one side over another. I have seen what damage 'political' priests do to a congregation, in creating division and misrepresenting Jesus' message.*

However, my favorite reflection is about a man named Colin. In his reflection on this everyman, Beresford gives us an *entrée* into the very heart of Jesus, our Christ, and our Savior, who uses each of us— sometimes the seemingly least likely—to be those through whom he proclaims to the world that he has come for all, saint and sinner alike. For it is in both saint and sinner that Jesus's message of love and peace resides:

> *Colin was a kind of saint—not a picture postcard one, but more of the down-to-earth kind. When I remember him, my feeling is one of gratitude. He helped me to get a little perspective on my own problems at a critical time in my life. I soon found a new job and a new direction. I learned that life goes on, as it does for Colin, who I pray now shares a heavenly home with the faithful departed in God's kingdom.*

What a gift! What a wonderful collection of reflections for me and for you, especially as we search everywhere for examples of God's love and peace in the world. Well, we can find those examples, and David Beresford gives us that pathway to look no further than our own backyard to be *Blessed By God.*

John C. Zagarella, O.Praem.
Daylesford Abbey
Paoli, PA

Preface

Blessed by God is a collection of meditations and essays on Christian life and faith. While some of the meditations were read by parishioners of the Church of the Messiah in 2023/4, most are appearing here for the first time. They contain theological reflections along with personal stories—as in life, there is no division between the divine and the ordinary.

One of the meditations is actually a long essay: "The Church and Communism." It began life as a short meditation for St. Martha's, Bethany Beach, and has been expanded to its current length. It is a much better piece of writing than before. The subject matter is not widely enough known and merits wider dissemination, which is why I have included it. However, within the overall theme of the book, it is like an oak tree in an apple orchard.

What does it mean to be blessed by God? Those seeking answers will, I hope, find some of them in this book. God's blessings are freely bestowed on believers and non-believers alike. The art of the Christian life is to recognize God's blessings and live into them, giving thanks to God for his providence and love.

Every book is a labor of love, and sharing this labor with me has been Ruth, my wife, who read the chapters and made critical suggestions. Again I am grateful to designer Bob Schwartz, who is responsible for the book's unique and beautiful style and layout. Finally, a warm thank you to my friend Nick Cerchio, who guided this book to publication.

Blessings magnify God's ineffable presence. May you come to know God's blessings in your own life and be a blessing to others.

David Beresford

December 2024

Blessed by God

Chapter 1

Jesus is a Good Teacher

I am grateful for the many teachers I have known throughout my life. Among them was Miss (later Dame) Sewell, who fired my life-long interest in drama and poetry. In Mr Baird's class, I learned French and gained an appreciation of French culture. An English teacher, Mr. Simms, suggested I create and edit a monthly school magazine. The magazine, called *Aftermath*, was printed on a hand-operated Gestetner and contained creative writings from fellow pupils.

Some teachers were memorable for the wrong reasons. My maths teacher had a habit of throwing sticks of chalk at inattentive pupils. In primary school, I encountered a class teacher fond of using the cane. I thought then, and still do, that the man was a sociopath. However, in the strange way that God works, I learned Psalm 23 in his class. It was our morning hymn at the start of each school day.

Fortunately, the good teachers outnumbered the bad. A good teacher will bring out the best in you and make you realize that you understand more than you think you do. The best of them are wise and have a love for their pupils. Using that definition, we can say that Jesus was, and is, a good teacher.

One of the marks of a good teacher and, for that matter, a good friend, is that they do not always tell you what you want to hear. Jesus says to his followers, "Do not judge, so that you may not be judged"; "Love your enemies"; "Forgive those who sin against you." How many times? "Seventy times seven."

James Tissot, Jesus Teaches the People by the Sea (Jésus enseigne le peuple près de la mer), c. 1886 - 1896, opaque watercolor over graphite on gray wove paper, 6 11/16 × 9 1/4 in. (17 x 23 1/2 cm), Brooklyn Museum, New York.

Jesus mixed clear statements like these with parables, little stories that were like riddles to be solved. They revealed the life of heaven present in the everyday.

Jesus is himself a pupil of his heavenly Father. He says: "The words that I say to you I do not speak on my own; but the Father who dwells in me does his works." (John 14:10) The correctness of Jesus' teaching proceeds from his close and prayerful relationship to the Father.

Jesus left us no writings of his own; his teachings were conveyed through spoken words and actions. He wasn't teaching academic subjects, but life subjects: how to live right, how to live alongside your neighbor, how to live in the sight of God. Jesus loved to teach. Adults were the chief beneficiaries of his teaching, but he also had a special regard for children: "It is to such as these that the kingdom of heaven belongs." (Mark 10:14) Our successful reception of Jesus' teachings depends upon our accepting them with a child-like trust and curiosity. Children often ask "Why?" That is how they learn, by asking and listening to the answers.

When we do the same, it is to form us into mature and adult Christians. Once you absorb Jesus' teachings and live by them, the benefit accrues not only to yourself but to the whole of society. The fruits of Christian teaching are called virtues: the seven classical ones are wisdom, fortitude, temperance, justice, faith, hope, and love.

We call Jesus Lord and Savior, but to his disciples, he was known as "Rabbi"—i.e., "Teacher." Jesus is our rabbi for life. Christians never stop learning because Jesus never stops teaching. Jesus calls upon his followers to be "perfect" (Matthew 5:48), which seems impossible until you realize that what he is saying is that you will always have more to learn. Perfection is never achieved in one lifetime; while Jesus is teaching us how to live in the present world, he is preparing us for life in the world to come.

Jesus is more than a good teacher, however. He is my companion who travels with me. I turn to him in times of greatest need. On the occasions when life starts to fall apart, Jesus is my rock. He teaches me resilience and not to take myself too seriously. He punctures my pride, which keeps wanting to rise up. He teaches me to love and to seek the truth, no matter how messy or inconvenient it may be.

Jesus is the soul of the world who fills me with compassion for others and suspends my judgment of them; I know Jesus is close when I am acting outside of my normal judgmental self. Jesus teaches me to have ambition—for the Church, for the kingdom of God, for my own salvation. Jesus teaches me through his saints, both dead and alive.

I could say more, but there would be no end to my telling. Jesus is my friend who has given me the vocation of a priest and evangelist. I know no finer life than the Christian life—something I often say to others. As he taught me, so I teach others, in my own imperfect way, with a heart for those who are seeking life and truth.

Chapter 2

Does God exist?

On a stormy night in June, 2013, a thirty-meter-high wind turbine in Bradworthy, Devon, crashed to the ground. According to National Wind Watch, the turbine had succumbed to "high winds on Saturday night." Two days later, the same thing happened. Another turbine, two hundred yards away, toppled into a muddy field. Built to last twenty-five years, the turbines managed less than three. In his Daily Telegraph column, journalist and staunch windfarm opponent James Delingpole argued that if proof were needed of God's existence, then here it was.

The newspaper article was tongue-in-cheek, although for some it struck a chord. If God can use earthquakes and lightning strikes to show his displeasure, then why not high winds? It all made perfect sense, especially if you thought windfarms were an unseemly blight on the landscape.

What is our criteria for proving God's existence? The comedian Woody Allen once remarked "If only God would give me some clear sign! Like making a large deposit in my name at a Swiss bank." A friend related the time when, in Yorkshire, England, he attended a large mega-church where the pastor drove his Ferrari onto the stage in the worship hall. The message was clear: with faith as strong as mine, this car could be yours. It was a tempting offer. People would love to believe in a God who has their best interests at heart. The truth is that God does, only not on our terms.

Those wanting a more authentic experience of God would be better off talking with members of the church. After a while, they would notice that faith is not equally held and that there is both an individual and a common faith.

Those with no faith are like toddlers learning to walk, supported and encouraged by those whose faith has grown into maturity. In conversation with the atheist Richard Dawkins, former Archbishop of Canterbury Rowan Williams observed:

> *Religion has always been a matter of community building, a matter of building relations of compassion, fellow-feeling and, dare I say it, inclusion…The notion that religious commitment can be purely a private matter is one that runs against the grain of religious history.*[1]

You can try finding God on your own, but you won't get very far. In his book "*All Christians are Monks*", George Guiver questions whether "in order to engage with Christ we think we need to be convinced by some beliefs first." Some of this is rooted in individualism, in the idea that being a Christian is a "personal project" and not one grounded in community life. Although the strength of one's personal faith can fluctuate, the church is a store of faith that can sustain the doubtful believer. He writes,

> *When I pray, my faith goes up and down, but that's OK, because I am carried by the faith of the church—all carrying each other, our boat held in its course by the wind of the Holy Spirit.*[2]

Before we ask the question, "Does God exist?" perhaps we should be asking another question, such as "How does one believe in God?" The author C.S. Lewis wrote:

> *There are certain things in Christianity that can be understood from the outside, before you have become a Christian. But there are a great many things that cannot be understood until you have gone a certain distance along the Christian road. Whenever you find any statement in Christian writings which you can make nothing of, do not worry. Leave it alone. There will come a day, perhaps years later, when you suddenly see what it meant.*[3]

Luca Giordano (Naples 1634 - Naples 1705), *The Conversion of Saint Paul*, c. 1690, Musée des Beaux-Arts, Nancy, France.

One may also reasonably ask, "Does the universe possess a spirit or intelligence or energy beyond ourselves, or is there only humanity and the rest of creation?" People of faith believe that the energy or spirit that creates, animates, and sustains the whole of the universe is God. Human beings can know this energy or spirit because each person possesses an inborn antenna for it. At first, the signals are faint but, over time, they grow louder and louder until it becomes impossible to ignore them.

Believing in God can be difficult because God is, to some extent, hidden from us. But God is also a God of revelation, not fully in one moment, but over the course of a lifetime. Even St. Paul, who heard the Lord speaking to him on the road to Damascus, did not acquire a fully developed belief because of that one encounter. He was blinded in his first meeting with Jesus and needed the assistance of fellow travelers. When Paul arrived in Damascus, a disciple named Ananias had to take him in (reluctantly) and look after him.

Paul's initial blindness is a metaphor for the person who cannot see God. Ananias showed hospitality to Paul, the persecutor of Christians, because the Lord had spoken to him. If you are looking for proof of God's existence, you will find it in the lives of people like Ananias. In the ancient world, Christians acquired a reputation for charity and kindness because they helped everyone, regardless of wealth or status.

Through the lives and witness of those who follow Jesus, many have come to know God. Christians draw their strength and inspiration from both Christ and the community. Belief is thus not simply a matter of faith but of *belonging*, as Rowan Williams and George Guiver identified.

An early Christian offers this advice: "Draw near to God, and he will draw near to you." (James 3:8) If God exists, he is not some remote deity who looks on the world from afar with bemused detachment. While God is found in community, he has a personal care and love for each person. God knew us even before we were born, when he "created my inmost self, knit me together in my mother's womb" (Psalm 139:13). God reaches out to the faithful and atheist alike, in their need and vulnerability. God "is near to all who call on him." (Psalm 145:18)

God exists. We know it not by his knocking down windmills but by those whose lives he has touched, healed, and drawn together in love. This is the God who has been recognized and believed in throughout the ages.

Notes

1.   "Richard Dawkins attacks 'irrelevant' religion in Rowan Williams debate", *Daily Telegraph*, February 1, 2013. <https://www.telegraph.co.uk/news/religion/9841063/Richard-Dawkins-attacks-irrelevant-religion-in-Rowan-Williams-debate.html#:~:text=In his address, Lord Williams, dare I say it, inclusion> [accessed December 6, 2024].

2.   George Guiver, *All Christians Are Monks*, (Durham: Sacristy Press, 2024), 48.

3.   C. S. Lewis, *Mere Christianity* (London: Harper Collins, expanded edition 2001), 144.

Chapter 3

What Does the Cross Do?

My wife Ruth was reading a story to our three-year-old granddaughter, who suddenly noticed the cross that Ruth was wearing.

"What is this?" she asked.

Ruth replied, "It's a cross."

"What does it do?"

Before I share with you the answer Ruth gave, I want to commend to your attention thewonderful theological question just posed by a three-year-old. I don't recall ever hearing this question before, not even at seminary, but it strikes me as an obvious and essential one. The cross: what does it do?

Ruth answered, "It reminds me of God's love for me". Behind that truth lies a powerful story of death and transformation.

The cross, as it was used in Roman times, was a means of execution. Everyone in first century Palestine knew exactly what the cross could do. After the crucifixion of Jesus Christ, however, the cross could do something else. It could touch the human heart.

The cross has never lost its original meaning and intention. Love and death both emanate from the cross. For the disciples, the death of Jesus on the cross was the end of a dream. The dark sky that hung over Jesus on the day of crucifixion brooded over the disciples in the following days.

Then, on the third day, Jesus was raised from the dead. The power of the cross was suddenly overtaken by the power of resurrection. In light of the resurrection, we may ask the same question, "What does the cross do?" The cross killed Jesus, but not forever. Ultimately, the cross failed in what it was meant to do.

The cross that we wear as a symbol of our Lord is a sign of God's victory over death, which he won through suffering and self-sacrifice. Through this supreme act of love, Jesus has transformed the cross into a sign of love, thereby robbing it of its human power over us. The human-shaped cross, the feared means of death, has become the symbol of God's love and reconciliation.

I leave you with another question, (although not as profound as the one my granddaughter asked). What does the cross mean to you?

Praise

Ask any church member why they go to church and they might say, "I go to church to hear God's word and receive communion." Alternatively, they might answer, "I like the music and the singing." Some might declare, "I want to take part in the life and mission of the church." One member told me, with some honesty, "I only go to church to see my friends." (I hope he included Jesus.)

Churches attract members and non-members alike. In my last church, meals for the poor were cooked by both. In fact, the church welcomes all people; from the priest to the acolyte, from the bell ringer to the flower arranger, church life involves people of different ages and status. Seen from the outside, churches appear a hive of activity. Yet there is one element that binds them all together. In fact, without this additional ingredient, the life and work of a church is incomplete. This additional, essential element is *praise*.

Praise is primarily a function of worship. Every Sunday, praise directs the church's life and intentions toward God. St. Augustine wrote that "the praise of God should be the object of our meditation in this life, because in the life of the world to come it will be forever the object of our rejoicing." The practice of praise therefore unites our intentions and equips us for the life hereafter, as well as directing our hearts and minds in the here and now.

Easter at Christ Church Christiana Hundred, Wilmington. Photo: Deborah Webb.

In praise, we express our *gratitude*. Out of a grateful heart, one praises God, even in the face of difficulties and defeats. Not surprisingly, a service of thanksgiving—the Eucharist—is the chief act of worship for most liturgical churches. The Greek word *eucharistia* means "Thanksgiving". In the eucharistic prayer, the priest exhorts the congregation to "Lift up your hearts." Thankful praise transcends worldly concerns as our hearts are lifted toward God.

It is fair to ask why praise is necessary. Does God need our praise? It's not as if God needs someone to tell him he is doing a good job. So why do we do it? We can ask this same question of ourselves. "Why do we praise others?" Praise is essentially an act of affirmation. By praising another we are affirming them for who they are and what they are doing.

The people who understood this were the ancient Israelites. They praised God daily by reciting poetry from a book called *Tehillim*, a Hebrew word which means *Praises*. It is better known to Christians as the Book of Psalms. In the psalms, God is praised throughout as the one who "delivers my soul from death, and my feet from falling, so that I may walk before God in the light of life." (Psalm 56:13).

If praise lies at the heart of a church's life, how do we measure its health and vitality? Praise grows from the regular practice of prayer. As worship is the external expression of the inner life of prayer, so the praise that flows from worship and prayer is carried into the day-to-day business of the church. This is because God wishes to consecrate the whole of the church's life. For this reason, the non-worship activities of the church cannot be considered as separate from worship and prayer, but as proceeding from them.

Sometimes, activities spring up that may not owe their origin to the prayer and worship life of the church. Some become established because someone thought it was a good idea at the time. It is easy to mistake a church's "busyness" for godly activity. But this is like admiring a beehive for its bees, rather than for the honey it produces. The church's praise is like honey from the hive. Its sweetness is a sign of God's presence. It is always better, before beginning any new work, mission, or ministry, to ask the question: "Is this God's will for the church or our own will?" The plans of humanity do not always align with God's plan. We must make sure that we praise God and not ourselves.

The office of Morning Prayer begins: "Lord, open our lips. And our mouth shall proclaim your praise." This sets the pattern for the church's worship throughout the day. In the poem Praise (II), George Herbert describes the life of one who daily praises God,

> *Sev'n whole dayes, not one in seven,*
> *I will praise thee.*
> *In my heart, though not in heaven,*
> *I can raise thee.*

In devotion and worship our lives are being shaped by praise. In turn, our praise brings blessings from God in an expanding circle of love. If we practice it often enough, praise becomes second nature. It connects us to God in a deeper way, which strengthens the life of the believer and the witness of the church.

Chapter 5

Julian of Norwich

The eleventh-century cathedral of the Most Holy Trinity in the city of Norwich, England, is one of the finest cathedrals in all of Europe. It stands in a close of around 44 acres and is surrounded by winding medieval streets and alleys. Over the centuries it has weathered riots, the Reformation, and natural disasters—in AD 1463 the spire burned down after being struck by lightning. Today the cathedral is a haven of peace and prayerfulness.

Among the stained glass windows that adorn the cathedral is one dedicated to a lady known as Julian. She takes her name from a nearby church - St. Julian's - where she lived as an anchoress. To be an anchorite or anchoress was a special calling. Most resided in a small cell attached to the side of the church. Their lives were devoted to prayer and adoration; there was usually a narrow space between the church and the cell—called the "sacrament squint"—through which the occupant of the small "ankerhold" could view the high altar and follow the daily worship of the Mass. In the fourteenth century, Julian was one of around 200 anchorites in the British Isles.

Julian lived in interesting times. In the 1340s, half of the population was wiped out by the bubonic plague. Julian was also alive during the Peasants' Revolt in 1381. During her lifetime she was known for her wisdom; people would visit her for advice and spiritual direction. She is known to us today as the author of the *Revelations of Divine Love*, an account of her visions

Wall plaque on St. Julian's Church, Norwich, UK.

which she received after long and intense periods of prayer. The Revelations were only published in the nineteenth century, but have since had a lasting impact on Christian theology and practice.

Julian had a holy desire to understand the nature of reality, and she prayed ardently; many of her revelations came after she had been, in effect, "pestering" God, who rewarded her persistence by sharing with her many of the secrets of the world. One of the most well-known of Julian's revelations concerns her meditation on a hazelnut. Here's an extract from the relevant passage (with the Old English updated for modern ears):

> *And in this he showed me something small, no bigger than a hazelnut, lying in the palm of my hand, as it seemed to me, and it was as round as a ball. I looked at it with the eye of my understanding and thought: What can this be? I was amazed that it could last, for I thought that because of its littleness it would suddenly have fallen into*

nothing. And I was answered in my understanding: It lasts and always will, because God loves it; and thus everything has been through the love of God. In this little thing I saw three properties. The first is that God made it, the second is that God loves it, the third is that God preserves it. But what did I see in it? It is that God is the Creator and the protector and the lover. For until I am substantially united to him, I can never have perfect rest or true happiness, until, that is, I am so attached to him that there can be no created thing between my God and me.

In this "shewing", as she called it, the hazelnut stands for her own love of God, which is small in the general scheme of things. But God reveals to her that her love is, in fact, no small thing, and that she holds in her hand a universe of love that permeates all of creation. Her desire is common to all mystics—that of union with God. Actually, it is a characteristic of all Christian love that we are to be united with the source of love itself.

St. Julian's church, where Julian is thought to have lived, was destroyed by German bombers during the Second World War. After the war, the church was rebuilt, along with a side chapel where Julian's cell would have been.

I was among a group of pilgrims who visited the church in 2022. On arrival, we were greeted by the Rector, who sat us down and gave us a short lecture on Julian. Afterward, he invited us to take a hazelnut from a basket on the table of the cell, and we prayed together in silence. The hazelnut is a surprisingly effective aide to prayer; the practice of holding a hazelnut in your palm and focusing on it helps to still the mind.

Afterward, I reflected on Julian's gift of herself and on the ardor of her love for God. How marvelous of God to return Julian's love by opening her mind to know the ways of God! In her visions, Julian discovered a God who was a creator, protector, and lover. As Julian held the hazelnut in her hand, she understood how God holds us in his.

Chapter 6

A Witness in Time

The ancient church of St. Botolph's, in West Sussex, England, dates from AD 950. My wife and I visited the church during a visit to the UK in 2024. In its current manifestation, the church building is of flint-rubble construction and incorporates additions and repairs from across the centuries. The western window dates from the late Saxon period of the eleventh century, while the eastern window was installed in the fourteenth century. The south porch dates from the nineteenth century.

There is evidence that the interior of the church was once covered with wall paintings. In the twelfth century, Cluny Abbey in France sent skilled artists across the English Channel to paint the interiors of English churches. These traveling artists adorned the walls of rural churches with a frieze of New Testament characters along with depictions of the saints. Almost nobody owned books then, so the vividly painted walls served up theology and evangelism in pictorial form.

Sited near the river Adur, the village of Botolphs was once a prosperous and well-populated area—at least, according to the Domesday survey from 1086. However, over the next five hundred years the area experienced a decline and in 1526 the impoverished parish was united with Bramber, a village about half a mile north. History has not delivered to us any startling revelations about St. Botolph's church. Archbishop Laud, who was

St. Botolph's Church, Botolphs, West Sussex, UK.

appointed by King Charles I, is believed to have preached once from its Jacobean pulpit. Otherwise, St. Botolph's is a quiet place where God invites us to enter and be still.

I remember worshiping here many years ago, when my friend, the Rector, invited me to attend the monthly Sunday eucharist. There were around twenty congregants in church that day. Most had come from the nearby farms, for whom the church was a local landmark and a reminder of God's presence. We heard the Scripture and then, after the eucharistic prayer, we received the sacrament. Our worship that morning united us to one another, and also to Christians worshiping in cathedrals, suburban churches, and country churches across the land.

I have always enjoyed the humble worship of a country church. In England, such churches are especially lively during harvest time, when vegetables of all descriptions are placed around the altar, and God is praised for his providence.

The local community gives thanks for the bounty of the earth and acknowledges God's blessing upon them. From heaven comes the blessing, and from earth comes the food; the people depend on both for their spiritual growth and survival.

Harvest Festival is a reminder that almost everything we eat depends on the land—the good soil provides the crops and feeds the animals. St. Botolph's church rests on the good soil of the earth and points to heaven. Amid the sway of the seasons and the daily struggle to survive, St. Botolph's stands as a silent witness to the partnership between God and his people.

What of the future of St. Botolph's, and the many churches like it, which once served growing populations but have now become historic landmarks? In 2013 St. Botolph's was declared "redundant" and placed under the care of the Churches Conservation Trust. Happily, the church remains open for prayer and in summer services are still held there. When we visited, the church was in remarkably good condition, considering its age.

Apart from worship, the church serves another useful purpose: it prompts us to reflect upon the passage of time. Through invasions, wars, changes in government, plagues, and persecutions, the church draws us back in time to imagine the lives of our ancestors. How did they live? By working the land and applying themselves to a life of physical labor. Life was centered around the village and the farm. Few would risk venturing beyond the safety of their known environment. Life was shorter then and families were larger, if only for economic reasons. From those faded wall paintings, one knew that death was the door to either eternal life or eternal damnation, depending on how you lived on earth.

After my wife and I left the church, we stopped outside and took some photos. On a cold winter's day, the church's tower caught the light of the low winter sun. There was something timeless about this scene. We then walked along the riverside path back to our car. Since our visit, St. Botolph's church has continued to travel with me. When I think of it, I am surprised at how, in its silence, the church has something to say to me.

Chapter 7

Evensong and Caviar

Nestled in the foothills of the South Downs, England, is the ancient village church of St John's, Bury. It is one of four churches in a parish located in the West Sussex countryside. The churches are surrounded by woodland and wetland, heath and scrub, with the river Arun running the length of the parish. In 2012 I was lucky enough to serve there as a curate. So beautiful is this area, with its abundant bird and wildlife, I nicknamed it "Eden".

On a return visit, my wife and I visited our friend Liz, who has lived in Bury for over forty years. Her sixteenth-century home has a thatched roof, with walls made of flint, brick, and stone, held up by oak and elm timbers. The house has its own personality and shifts and creaks according to the seasons. On the walls of the dining room are antique icons that face one another, like guests at a dinner party. The icons were acquired by Liz's late husband while on business in Greece and Russia. When I was researching icons for a talk at St John's, Liz let me study them. When I eventually left the parish, she kindly made a present of one of them—The Harrowing of Hell—which now hangs on the wall of my home in the USA.

When I first arrived in Bury, I was told that it existed in a bubble from the 1950s—an exaggeration, no doubt, but there was an element of truth in it. The close proximity of old churches and castles lends a timeless feel

Harrowing of Hell (Russian eighteenth century).

to the place. With its rural setting and slower pace of life, one could live there without being unduly disturbed by events in the outside world. Changes to village life usually revolved around people being born, dying, or moving house.

St. John's, Bury, Pulborough, West Sussex, UK.

The churches in the parish, which date from the eleventh to the thirteenth century, are: St John's, Bury; St Giles, Coldwaltham; St Botolph's, Hardham; and St Nicholas, Houghton. The Rector has the cure of all four churches. On Sunday morning, he or she takes a service in one church and then moves on to the next. It is unusual to do all four in one morning, but it happened to me one Sunday. Three eucharists at three churches, finishing with a baptism at St. John's at 12:15 pm. By then, I should have felt exhausted, but with the adrenaline flowing, I could have done all four again.

When the churches were built, most people lived in the countryside, and each church had its own minister. On Sunday nearly everyone in the village and neighboring farms went to church. Today it is a different story. The number of regular worshippers attending church has fallen dramatically.

St. Nicholas, Houghton, West Sussex, UK.

The Industrial Revolution in the nineteenth century sparked the drift of populations into cities and, more recently, the growth of secularism has reduced the size of congregations. People have learned to get along without Christianity. I could say "without religion", but secularism has its own religions, and people tend to follow the ones of their own choosing.

Yet the village church continues to fulfill the same purpose it did hundreds of years ago: to provide a spiritual home for a worshiping community. Sometimes there are two opportunities for worship on a Sunday: a Eucharist in the morning and an Evensong at night.

So it was for us, when Liz invited us to stay for Evensong at St. Nicholas church in the neighboring village of Houghton (Liz pronounces it "Hoe'-tun"). Without wishing to sound uncharitable, Houghton is one of those "blink and you'll miss it" places. In the seventeenth century, King Charles II is said to have stopped briefly at Houghton's pub, the George and Dragon, whilst being pursued by Parliamentary soldiers. (He is also said to have hidden in a tree in Southwick, some twenty miles away). St. Nicholas church dates from the thirteenth century, although its present appearance owes much to those indefatigable rebuilders, the Victorians.

The church lies on the slope of a hill beside a neighboring farm. While its doors are closed during winter, in summer and fall there are regular services. Evensong on Sunday was at 6:00 pm and we arrived ten minutes early. The farm owners next door had given permission for parking near the cattle shed. The dirt path to the church door was lit on either side by tea lights set in the grass verge. Upon entering the church, we were greeted by a mixture of faces old and new. There's something unique about the tradition of Evensong in the Church of England. The outside world, with its constant demands and interruptions, disappears whenever worshippers are enveloped in the timeless beauty of Evensong in an English country church.

The service began with a hymn, and the sound of the organ was one I recognized—it was the same one I heard when I was a curate, and it was still being operated by the same person, Mike, the churchwarden of St. Botolph's. Actually, the organ was not an organ but a music amplifier of indeterminate vintage which I had nicknamed "Mr Sony." Hearing it again, I was reminded of its peculiar foible, which was an inability to provide a pause at the end of a line of music. That meant you had to take a breath when you could, which required the omission of words as you were singing. Fortunately, as we all took breaths at different times, no one noticed.

The Rector was away that Sunday and the service was taken by the Reverend Canon John Bundock, who was visiting from outside of the benefice. He preached a sermon on *The Lord of the Dance* and told us how we need to listen to the tune God is playing and learn to dance in step. At the end of the service, Canon John announced that, for those who wished to stay, wine and cheese would be served at the back of the church. He added that a member of the congregation had just returned from a trip to Russia and had brought caviar to share with everyone. Caviar? At Evensong in a village church? I noticed that nobody left the church. Instead, people began to form an orderly line in front of the fish roe and crackers. By the time I got there, the crackers were all gone, and most of the caviar, but I managed to scoop out a dab of the black stuff using a stick of celery.

Caviar and Evensong would make an interesting story for a stewardship campaign. Praise God in worship and offer caviar to the faithful. But wait—

wouldn't some people consider caviar a needless extravagance? Wouldn't that money have been better spent? I thought of the generosity of the person who brought it, and it reminded me of the generosity of Mary Bethany, who anointed Jesus' feet with expensive and fragrant nard (John 12:1-8). Her own loving act, which Jesus defended, mirrors the extravagant generosity of God's love.

The caviar was the best gift the man could bring to church that Sunday. He took pleasure in seeing the looks of surprise and delight on the faces of his fellow worshipers. We all felt a little spoiled, and our secret guilt made the caviar even more delectable. Did it detract from the worship? Only in the way that stained glass windows, or fine vestments, could. It was a variation on the theme of giving one's best to God. Imagine if everyone brought the best of themselves to church, or indeed to any situation? Imagine if, instead of arriving with the thin gruel of judgments, resentments, and envy, each of us brought the caviar of joy, hope, and gracious conversation?

Evensong at St. Nicholas in Houghton was the perfect end to our leisurely Sunday. It combined worship and hospitality—an irresistible combination, in my opinion. Like caviar at Evensong, God's blessings can be a powerful and pleasant surprise in the midst of our humdrum, day-to-day existence. God is a generous giver, who shares his life with us in Jesus Christ. Learning to give the best of what you have is the proper way to live out your faith. And, as you do, God always adds a little something.

Our fellow worshiper—the one who brought the caviar—blessed us with his generosity. In the timelessness of Evensong in an ancient village church, we heard God's voice and received a lesson in faith and giving.

Chapter 8

Home

Where is Home?

In the middle of the driveway lay a small bird's nest, around three inches wide, which had fallen from an overhanging tree. I stooped down to pick it up. In my hand the nest felt surprisingly heavy, with its carefully woven strands of dried grass making a perfect bowl. For some moments I stood admiring its construction. It was a wonder of intricate and delicate beauty.

Inside the nest there was a single white feather—the sign of a previous occupant? The nest was built for a purpose, which was to be a home. Humans often borrow terminology from the bird world when talking about "home". At some point in our own lives, we have "flown the nest." Many parents near retirement age are called "emptynesters." Pregnant mothers are said to possess a "nesting instinct", when they prepare a home for the arrival of their new baby.

I don't know what happens inside a bird's brain, however, I have a feeling that birds do not treat their nests with the same sentimentality human beings treat their homes. Birds' nests have a purely practical function: it is where chicks are born and raised. On the other hand, human beings think of home in both practical and emotional terms: it is the place of beginning and of return, even when "home" no longer exists.

Where is home for you? This question was posed to me by a complete stranger at a garden party in Bury, West Sussex. I had recently moved into the nearby vicarage, and the verger had invited me to a party at her house. To the question I replied, without a moment's hesitation, "home is about a mile away." The stranger probed me further. "Actually, that's not what I meant. Where is *home*?" As he stood there, I searched my mind but could only draw a blank. In the end I simply said, "home is where the heart is." Judging by the look on his face, the answer was obviously lacking. Ever since, I have pondered the question. Where *is* home? Or, *what* is home? Is home a place, or a memory? Does it exist now, or in the past?

There's a good reason why I found the original question difficult to answer. When I count the number of homes I have lived in since birth, it comes to over fifty. As a child, our family was always on the move.

My father, an airline executive, enjoyed steady promotion which involved us relocating from one company home to another. By the time I was fourteen, I had lived in five different homes in four different cities in two different countries. As children, home was wherever our parents happened to be. Later, as an adult, I continued the pattern set in childhood, of moving from home to home on a regular basis.

My clearest memories of childhood homes are between the ages of five and fifteen. I remember the houses and the streets, the gardens and the areas where we would find adventure as children. All of these places hold memories of my early social and emotional experiences. I could define these memories as "home", but that would not do justice to what I think "home" really means. Home is more than the sum of the places where I grew up, or the emotional and social experiences of youth. Home is a state of mind.

The Swedish author Henning Mankel wrote that "You can have more than one home. You can carry your roots with you, and decide where they grow." I recently had dinner with a friend who, three years earlier, had moved from Springfield, Pennsylvania to Winter Haven, Florida. She moved to be close to her family. When I asked her, "Where is home?", she replied without hesitation, "Springfield." She explained that she had lived there most of her life. Her friends lived there: it was the place where she was married and had raised a child. Yet, if a policeman had stopped her and asked her for her home address, she would have said "Winter Haven."

For many people, "home" is a place of love and acceptance, where you are free to be yourself. Maya Angelou described home as "The safe place where we can go as we are and not be questioned." The ideal home is a place of welcome and of yearning, associated with ideas that reinforce our positive view of home. Think of sayings such as "the comfort of home", "home cooking," and "there's no place like home." Home is a place where we want to belong. However, this is not universally true. For some, home can be a place of dread or fear, especially in homes where there is violence, sexual abuse, or simply a feeling of being trapped. For people who live in homes like these, it can be hell on earth.

Leaving Home

A proper understanding of "home" matters to us, because it helps us to know who we are. Paradoxically, our self-knowledge often develops only when we have left home. In our myths and legends, from the *Odyssey* to *The Lord of the Rings*, home has an essential but small part to play. It is a place of beginning and, sometimes, a place of ending, but it is seldom, at least in narrative terms, a place of much interest. Home has a passive role to play in our human story. Like birds flying the nest, human beings need to leave home in order to find new life outside. It is the difference between home and what lies beyond which makes our human story interesting.

The guitarist Duane Allman was the leader of the Allman Brothers Band. Less than a year before his tragic death in September 1971, he was interviewed for a radio broadcast. At the time the band was continually touring. Asked if he ever got the chance to live at home, Allman replied, "Gypsies ain't got no home, I'm at home when I'm with my people; I'm always at home, I'm home now."

Leaving home is either an adventure or a trauma, or both. The Bible offers plenty of examples. Consider Adam and Eve, who are expelled from their home—the Garden of Eden—and must fend for themselves in the world outside. Exile from home is the price they pay for disobeying God. It is a catastrophe for them because, outside of the garden, they are no longer immortal. Home was where they could live in innocence forever and want for nothing. It all sounded perfect. Yet we can observe that the home from which they were banished was hardly the paradise we imagine it to be. After all, it contained a serpent who deceived the couple into disobeying God.

Consider, too, the stories of Moses, Abraham, Jacob, Joseph, and Daniel, all of whom leave home, either by choice or as exiles. In each case, separation from home is the catalyst that enables their own characters to be tested and developed. Away from family and friends, they discover inner resources to overcome the difficulties they face. Equally importantly, they rely on God's providence for their survival.

In the gospels, leaving home is the sacrifice the disciples make in order to follow Jesus. Peter says to Jesus, "Look, we have left our homes and followed you." (Luke 18:28) It could be said that Jesus himself left home when he came down from heaven to live on earth. As an adult, Jesus was homeless. He once said, "Foxes have holes, and birds of the air have nests; but the Son of Man has nowhere to lay his head." (Matthew 8:20)

A Home in Heaven

In Jesus, we follow the life of an itinerant preacher and prophet, who travels by foot over the vast, dusty plains and mountains of ancient Palestine, visiting towns and villages and encountering people on their home turf. Jesus has only a short time to share the good news of God's kingdom breaking into the lives of his followers. The idea of "home" is embedded in this teaching, as a place in this world and in the world to come. At one point Jesus tells his disciples,

> *In my Father's house, there are many dwelling places. If it were not so, would I have told you that I go to prepare a place for you? And if I go and prepare a place for you, I will come again and will take you to myself, so that where I am, there you may be also. (John 14:2-3)*

Jesus is referring to their eternal home, which is life after death. He does not describe its physical trappings. Instead, he talks in terms of relationship: the words "I" and "you" are repeated a number of times. Heaven, therefore, is a place of companionship; Jesus is reassuring the disciples that death will not mean separation from him. What is notable about this passage is that the life after death that Jesus describes is not very different from their current lives. The place to which he refers will, therefore, be familiar to them.

The poet T. S. Eliot conveys this paradox in his poem Little Gidding.

We shall not cease from exploration
And the end of all our exploring
Will be to arrive where we started
And know the place for the first time.

This is consistent with the disciples' meetings with the resurrected Jesus. At first, they do not recognize him, yet after a while or even within moments, there is something that changes their perception of him. He is the same, yet different. Can we relate this change in perception to the difference between our earthly and heavenly homes? The disciples' heavenly home will be recognizable, but in a way that they will "know the place for the first time." The catalyst for this change of perception will be their relationship with Jesus.

A Home on Earth

We can define "home" as existing in two dimensions: earthly and heavenly. It is significant that as well as creating homes for ourselves to live in, we also make them for God. Although "heaven and the highest heaven cannot contain God" (1 Kings 8:27), Solomon built a temple as a home for God. A temple or a church is a kind of spiritual home on earth: we honor God by making a home where God can dwell, where the people assemble and are formed through worship into a holy community or family. The temple or church thus becomes the place where things earthly and heavenly are explicitly combined. We honor God through prayer and worship and God blesses and unites us through the power of love.

Temples and churches are therefore holy places, where heaven meets earth and where God and the faithful regularly gather. However, when we no longer honor God and care less for God's home than our own, God's anger will be kindled against us, and God's blessings will be withheld. The prophet Haggai spoke to God's people at a time when the Temple was neglected and God was not honored.

The word of the Lord came by the prophet Haggai, saying…Because my house lies in ruins, while all of you hurry off to your own houses, therefore the heavens above you have withheld the dew, and the earth has withheld its produce. (Haggai 1:3, 8-10)

God dwells within the walls of the church but is not confined there. God will make his home in the heart of a devout man or woman. St. Paul likens the body to our home on earth, so that even if this earthly home is destroyed, "we have a building from God, a house not made with hands, eternal in the heavens." (2 Cor. 5:1) St. Caesarius of Arles puts it thus: "God does not live only in shrines made by man, structures of wood or stone, but above all he lives in the soul which is made after his image."

My Home

When I was asked, "Where is home for you?" I replied, "Home is where the heart is."That clichéd statement contains a seed of truth.While my questioner was seeking an answer that located me in my place of origin, my own experience had led me to understand "home" rather differently. Being at home in the heart means living in places where love is given and received. If home is, as Jesus describes it, a place of relationship, then we are only truly at home in the presence of another.

There is always a balance to be struck. One can say, "I am at home with God when God makes a home in me." If we invite someone into our home, we usually make the effort to clean the house in order to make our guests feel comfortable. If we think of the church as a home, then the same rule applies. However, home is not where God and I dwell together alone. The value of home lies in its power to foster relationships. Home welcomes others.

Traditionally, "home" is where families are raised. Our sense of self— who we are—begins at home, through the love and nurture of parents and siblings. Home also takes in our surroundings: the terrain and landscape, whether urban or country. The church or temple is a family home of a different kind: larger, more diverse, yet essentially the same: it is the place where loving relationships are made and sustained.

Home is a place of refuge. Far from the physical home where one lives, far from the stability it provides, home abides in the human heart. The refuge who has left home or has lost their home will carry "home" with them in their heart. As the search for a physical home begins, the consciousness of their heavenly home increases. The desire for shelter and the desire for God increase in tandem with one another.

The small nest that I picked up from the driveway now sits on the window ledge in our kitchen. It serves to remind me that as fledglings we are launched into the world, carried either by the winds of the spirit or by our own endeavors. No longer confined by the walls of the nest, we can discover new relationships and challenges outside of our physical home. At the same time, through our relationship with God, we come to know another home. It is this home that we will enter at the end of our days and where, as the poet reminds us, we will "know the place for the first time."

Chapter 9

The Church and Communism

A good tree cannot bear bad fruit, nor can a bad tree bear good fruit.
Matthew 7:18-20

In June 2021, a delegation from the Chinese government, led by the new Chinese ambassador to the United Kingdom, Zheng Zeguang, visited the tomb of Karl Marx in Highgate Cemetery, London. The ambassador laid a wreath to celebrate the one hundredth anniversary of Chinese communism. In a speech beside the tomb, the ambassador told his listeners that Marxism "has led the Chinese people to overcome all difficulties and achieve enormous success in the new democratic revolution and the socialist revolution, development, and reform."

The visit of the Chinese delegation—following a well-worn path of previous visitations from communist dignitaries—is an example of how the religious impulse inherent in all people can find expression even in atheist ideology. One wonders if the Chinese delegation was aware that their visit had its corollary in the Christian practice of pilgrimage.

It is doubtful that Marx ever intended his plan to transform the economic, political, and social structures of the world to become a religious movement. In fact, he disparaged religion, describing it as "the heart of a heartless world." Friedrich Engels, who, with Marx, co-wrote *The Communist Manifesto*, saw religion as standing in the way of the new type of world he and Marx envisaged. In 1844 he wrote,

We want to sweep away everything that claims to be supernatural and superhuman...for that reason, we have once and for all declared

war on religion and religious ideas and care little about whether we are called atheists or anything else.[1]

Despite this assertion, communism has, whether intentionally or not, adopted some of the behaviors of a religious movement. For example, the use of processions with banners, along with speeches extolling the communist ideology, imitates ecclesiastical liturgy. The speeches of communist leaders are secular sermons, intended to educate the masses to the benefits of socialism. As for the banners, they carry images of the new saints: Marx, Engels, and Lenin (or Mao Zedong, in China.). In the Soviet Union, there was also a concerted effort by the authorities to replace church rituals, such as weddings, with self-styled atheistic ones. Although

Mikhail M. Cheremnykh. *You Are Waiting in Vain at the Church Door, Priest—We Live Wonderfully without Icons and God! (U tserkovnogo poroga zhdesh', pop, naprasno - bez ikon i boga my zhivem prekrasno!)*, 1939, poster, 27 × 42 in., published in Moscow, Soviet Union.

these new atheistic services were deemed to "occasionally lack emotionality and aesthetic appeal", nevertheless they "facilitated the displacement" of religious rituals "from the sphere of everyday life."[2]

The desire of communism to supplant religious practice entered the private as well as the public sphere. In communist Russia, the use of religious icons was widespread. Icons are devotional aids and usually depict the saints to whom the faithful pray to intercede on their behalf. At first, the State discouraged the use of icons and spread propaganda about them. A newspaper article from 1924 even claimed that kissing icons caused an outbreak of syphilis.[3] People were directed to replace icon corners with Godless or Lenin corners. The Godless Corner featured "photos, small exhibits, brochures, and a wall newspaper." A Lenin corner usually included "an array of pictures of Lenin at various stages of his life."[4]

If imitation is the sincerest form of flattery, then the most striking example is the preservation of Lenin's body in a specially built mausoleum in Red Square. This macabre display borrowed from the long-held belief in the Orthodox tradition that, when a saintly man or woman died, their sanctity was proven by the incorruptibility of their body after death. The government predictably denounced these religious phenomena; the Justice Department had declared that "The cult of dead bodies and these dolls must end." However, when Lenin died in 1924, the government quietly adopted the tradition, by embalming Lenin's body and placing it in a glass casket, where it could be viewed by millions of the communist faithful. There, in the hushed atmosphere of the tomb, the former leader lay miraculously preserved, not by grace, but by science.

Such practices highlight the inescapable fact that Communism and Christianity are rivals since both make similar claims about the religious sensibilities of human beings. The Catholic scholar Francis X Maier, in an article about the Italian intellectual, Del Noce, explained the religious appeal of Marxism.

> *It has powerful tools for social and economic analysis. It has a comprehensive anthropology—a vision of who and what a human being is—which claimed the mantle of science. And it has a religion-like, evangelical zeal that inspired the masses. As a result, it undermined biblical faith with a new, this-worldly, messianic gospel. In the Marxist canon there was good (the working class) vs. evil (capitalists), a path of redemption (revolution), the hope of heaven (a utopian future), and the certainty of final triumph (the direction of history)[5]*

This alternative system of salvation, based on the class struggle, seeks to replace Christianity's version, which follows Jesus' commandments to love

Unknown. Religion hinders the Five-Year Plan—Down with religious holidays—Join the League of Militant Atheists—Religion is a means of enslaving workers—All religions equally interfere and harm socialist construction, 1929, poster, 29 x 401/2 in., published in Leningrad, Soviet Union.

God and one's neighbor as oneself. In communist Russia, the government did not envisage a mutual co-existence with the historic Orthodox Church, seeing it as a relic of the old regime and an obstacle to political change. Communists set in motion plans for its destruction, which included the establishment of a rival organization called *The League of the Militant Godless*. The League was dedicated to mockery and hatred of God and of priests and believers.

At the same time, the State began to confiscate or destroy church property and raise taxes on priests. One of its greatest acts of sacrilege was the dynamiting (at night) of the Cathedral of Christ the Savior in Moscow. (The destruction of the church was filmed for posterity—an indication that the communists believed that they were making history).

However, the destruction of church property was soon surpassed by the murderous practices of the new regime. The killing of priests and others was undertaken with revolutionary zeal, encapsulated by Leon Trotsky, head of the Red Army, who said, "We must rid ourselves once and for all of the Quaker-Papist babble about the sanctity of human life."

Trotsky's outburst highlights a central feature of the new religion: its disdain for human life. Everything is subsumed to the cause of the revolution. Del Noce described it thus:

In Platonic-Christian thought, man is in a necessary relationship with God and in a contingent relationship with society…For Marxist atheism, the relationship with society becomes necessary and constitutive. Therefore in Marxism, the Christian subordination of politics to ethics must be replaced by the absorption of ethics into politics.[6]

In practical terms, communism justifies the use of terror against its populace by invoking the need to protect the people from its enemies. Who were the enemy? In communist Russia, it was the capitalists, kulaks, Cossacks, clergy, and counter-revolutionaries—in fact, the Bolsheviks needed an enemy in order to establish their own self-identity. The personal qualities and beliefs of individuals within each group were of no importance. When referring to the kulaks in 1934, the novelist Ilya Ehrenburg wrote, "Not one of them was guilty of anything, but they belonged to a class that was guilty of everything."[7]

Between 1917 and 1939, the numbers of those counted as "enemies" and put to death, either through starvation, as in the Ukraine, or by state-sanctioned murder, amounted to tens of millions. Life in communist Russia became increasingly bloody, reaching a peak of madness and brutality in the Great Terror of 1936-38 when over 700,000 people were murdered and many more exiled to camps or placed in prisons. Government documents record that in the Stalinist purges of 1937-38 alone, 106,000 Orthodox priests were slaughtered.[8] During this period, the communists also closed fourteen thousand churches and arrested thirty-five thousand "servants of religious cults."[9]

The sheer scale and pervasiveness of the terror is hard for modern readers to grasp. A climate of fear pervaded daily life, and those who considered themselves loyal apparatchiks were often victims. When arrested, they showed signs of surprise, saying "Zachto? Why? What for?"The poet Anna Akhmatova, however, understood precisely the reason, or rather, unreason. "Don't you understand," she said, "that they are now arresting people for nothing?" The violence and terror became an end in itself.[10]

Violence against the populace could be easily justified or rationalized, and there was no shortage of willing hands to serve the communists' ends. Aldous Huxley reminds us that

> *The surest way to work up a crusade in favor of some good cause is to promise people they will have a chance of maltreating someone…To be able to destroy with good conscience, to be able to behave badly and call your bad behavior 'righteous indignation'—this is the height of psychological luxury, the most delicious of moral treats.*[11]

In 1992, when I was the editor of St. Michael and All Angels magazine in Brighton, England, I discovered a stack of church magazines from the 1930s in a closet above the sacristy. Given their age, the magazines were in relatively good condition. In the December, 1931 edition of the magazine, there was a moving account of Christmas in Russia in 1930. As far as I am aware, this account has never been published before. Here is what it recorded:

> *In a letter written last Christmas by the daughter of a Russian priest to her brother in exile in England, I read these sentences: 'We had such a happy Christmas together, Grandmother and Grandfather, Father, Mother, the children'—her husband had been shot in the preceding November—'and I. The Godless made a great procession mocking us and stood outside the Church singing ribald songs and blaspheming the Savior and His Mother. But inside Father celebrated the Divine Liturgy. There were many there. We received the Holy Sacrament and knew that the blessed Lord was with us. The angels sang with us and so did Nikushka'—her husband—'and so did you. I knew it. Peace was in our hearts. We prayed lovingly for the Godless themselves.'*

> *'After the Liturgy we had dinner. For once there was plenty for the children. There was cabbage soup, and kind friends had given us eggs and cheese and bread. The Godless who had a great feast near our cottage came to mock our poverty. They had roasted a whole pig and had eaten many luxuries. They were very drunk. But we did not envy them—for in our hearts was Love and Goodwill to all and we were together. In the evening the O.G.P.U.'—the Soviet secret police— 'came and took Father away. They have sent him to the prison camp*

because the people love him. We are not afraid. They may kill his body but they cannot take his love from us. The Peace of Jesus is in our hearts and we trust him. Our Christmas was like heaven.'

This moving account, buried in an old church magazine, offers first-hand evidence of the authoritarian and anti-Christian nature of the communist regime. The full scale of the barbarity would only become apparent much later, in books such as Solzhenitsyn's The Gulag Archipelago, published in 1973. Yet the fact of a brutal regime murdering its own people was already well known at the time. In 1930, Pope Pius XI wrote an open letter condemning the persecution of Christians in Soviet Russia.

This was followed in 1937 by the encyclical DIVINI REDEMPTORIS, (Divine Redeemer) which condemned "atheistic communism as they are manifested chiefly in bolshevism." It identifies the dehumanizing nature of communism, which "strips man of his liberty, robs human personality of all its dignity, and removes all the moral restraints that check the eruptions of blind impulse." It also condemned "the conspiracy of silence on the part of a large section of the non-Catholic press of the world."

Why did Marxism attract such a strong following among journalists, artists, and writers? The author David Pryce-Jones notes that,

A mystery peculiar to the twentieth century is that intellectuals were eager to endorse the terror and mass-murder which characterized Soviet rule, at one and the same time abdicating humane feelings and all sense of responsibility towards others, and of course perverting the pursuit of truth.[12]

The appeal of communism had a strong religious component. After reading Marx, Engels, and Lenin, the author Arthur Koestler wrote that,

Something had clicked in my brain that shook me like a mental explosion. To say that one had 'seen the light' is a poor description of the mental rapture, which only the convert knows, regardless of what faith he has been converted to.[13]

The English poet Stephen Spender also extolled communism's religious dimension.

It is obvious that there were elements of mysticism in this faith. Indeed, I think that this is an attraction of communism for the

intellectual. To believe in political action and economic forces which will release new energies in the world is a release of energy in oneself.[14]

Other intellectuals and artists, including the poet Louis Aragon, playwright G B Shaw, and novelist Theodore Dreiser, championed the benefits of communist rule while turning a blind eye to the murderous excesses of the regime. Many visited the USSR to see for themselves how communism was transforming humankind for the better. In her book Western Intellectuals and the Soviet Union, Professor Ludmilla Stern wrote about these visits:

> *For Communists and fellow-travelers—non-party members sympathetic to the Communist cause—the trip to the USSR indeed had an air of sanctity about it. For the as yet unconverted, it was a quest for truth, a matter of intellectual integrity.*[15]

The visits were carefully orchestrated by the Soviet authorities, and the visitors saw what they wanted to see. The co-opting of artists and intellectuals into promoting the communist ideal was all part of the deception. Trotsky called them *poputschiki*, or "fellow travelers".[16.] Another phrase, attributed to Lenin, describes them as "useful idiots." The willingness of these "idiots" to suppress facts in the cause of a higher "truth" raises interesting psychological questions. Western communists saw themselves as having a higher calling, as agents fighting for a better society. But by willfully ignoring the suffering and deaths of millions, the Western intellectuals had effectively surrendered their own moral and intellectual integrity to a murderous political ideology.

Although Marxism grew out of the Enlightenment and claimed a basis in rational thought, it was rooted in the seductive idea of creating a new world order. David Horowitz, who was raised a communist but later renounced his "faith", explains the anthropological dimension of Marxist thought:

> *The revolutionary idea was not to attain a new place in the old order of things, but to change the world itself. Marxism was about a new creation that would begin with a "new man" and "new woman." It was about remaking the world. About going back to Eden and beginning again. It was the romance to end all romances.*[17]

While many were prepared to go along with the deception, others recorded the truth as they saw it. The American anarchist Emma Goldman spent two years in Russia and had plenty of time to observe the regime at close quarters. Deported by the US government for sedition in 1919, she arrived at her birthplace, Russia, as a firm believer in revolution, and as an exile from capitalist America. She was thus able to circulate freely in communist circles and at one point even met Lenin. Yet by 1920 she became disheartened about the regime and its excesses. In her book, *My Disillusionment in Russia*, published in 1923, she records the practices of the

Unknown. Religion is poison. Protect the children. 1930, poster, published in the Soviet Union

Cheka—the secret police—including mass arrests, beatings, torture, and execution of citizens. When she criticized these practices to a communist official, he replied, "You should be ashamed of yourself; you, an old revolutionist, and yet so sentimental." She commented:

> *During the past several months I had come to realize that the Communists believed any suggestion of the value of human life, quality of character, the importance of revolutionary integrity as the basis of a new social order, was repudiated as 'bourgeois sentimentality,' which had no place in the revolutionary scheme of things.*[18]

Radicals like Goldman and Horowitz became disillusioned because they assumed, wrongly, that communism came with a personal moral code. In theory, Lenin denounced traditional ethics "given to it by the bourgeoisie, who based ethics on God's commandments". "Communist morality", Lenin explained to a gathering of the Youth League in October 1920, "is entirely subordinated to the interests of the proletariat's class struggle." Lenin explicitly rejected any morality "based on extra-human [i.e. Godly] and extra-class concepts." Communism removed morality from the divine and personal realm and relocated it to the state.

In practice, Lenin's reframing of morality has been a disaster for humanity. Wherever communism is practiced, whether in Russia, China, or elsewhere, it involves the suppression of individual freedoms and, in most cases, mass murder. A glance through history provides unmistakable evidence: in every communist country, from Cambodia to Cuba, communism is the enemy of the human soul. Its fruits are the submissive compliance of the media, the rewriting of history, the growth of government corruption and bureaucracy, the imprisonment of those critical to the regime, and a population overseen by a handful of elites who enrich themselves at the expense of others.

In Russia, communism's challenge to the church faltered with the German invasion of 1941. Stalin realized that in order to defeat Hitler he would need the support of the Church. In 1943 he disbanded *The League of Militant Godless* and met with leaders of the Orthodox Church. The two sides remained uneasy allies until 1959 when Khrushchev launched a fresh attack against the Church. Christians could only worship publicly if they did not question the government. It continued in this way until the fall of the Soviet Union in 1991.

The end of Soviet communism was a cause for rejoicing, yet communism itself was not defeated. The other great communist country was China, whose death toll in the years following their revolution exceeded even that of the Soviet Union. The former Chinese leader Mao Zedong attempted to eliminate Christianity altogether, which survived as an underground movement, only for it to re-emerge in the 1980s under Deng Xiaoping. Today, there are estimated to be fifty million Christians in China, but the current Premier Xi Jinping is gradually increasing his control over the way Christianity is regulated and practiced. The human rights activist Benedict Rogers described the current situation:

> *Every church is now forced to demonstrate its loyalty to the CCP by displaying portraits of Xi Jinping and party propaganda banners alongside, or even instead of, religious images. Surveillance cameras are prohibited from going into places of worship at all. Meanwhile, are installed at the altar, recording all who attend, while under-18s Christians on low incomes have been pressured by officials to give up their faith, with threats that their state support could be withheld.[19]*

In 2018, the Roman Catholic Church came to an agreement—the text of which remains secret—with the Chinese government. With the intention

Worshippers in a Roman Catholic church in China.

of safeguarding the church, Pope Francis allowed the Chinese Communist Party to nominate new bishops for final approval by the Pope. In return, Catholics who had been imprisoned were expected to be released. However, that did not happen—indeed, in an Order (No. 15) issued in 2021 by the Chinese government, China gave itself the power to choose bishops without reference to the Pope. In October 2022, an appeasement minded Vatican renewed the agreement, although it is hard to explain why, since the Chinese government continues to crack down on religious freedom.

Given the history of communism—no political system in human history has killed more people—it is surprising to learn that, for many in the West, Marxism remains a valid alternative to capitalism. Today, its champions can be found in our higher learning institutions, in some social action groups, and even within the judicial and executive offices of the government. Given the antagonism of communism to the Christian faith, it is also surprising to find advocates for communism among the clergy and theologians.

A past example of clergy advocacy for communism was the Rev. Hewlett Johnson, Dean of Canterbury Cathedral from 1931-1963. Nicknamed "the Red Dean", in 1939 he published *The Socialist Sixth of the World*, a critique of capitalism as a "doomed" economic system which created inequalities of wealth. Soviet communism, on the other hand, delivered a kind of utopia, where everyone had a share in ownership and industry and "everyone had

The Chinese national flag flies in front of St Joseph's Church, also known as Wangfujing Catholic Church, in Beijing on Oct. 22, 2020, the day a secretive 2018 agreement between Beijing and the Vatican was renewed for another two years.

their rightful place in the labor force."[20] Johnson concluded his book by stating that

> *The communist puts the Christian to shame in the thoroughness of his quest for a harmonious society. Here he proves himself to be heir of the Christian intention.*[21]

Johnson's book became a minor bestseller, and in 1951 the Soviet Union awarded him the Stalin Peace Prize. The book exists today as a curiosity. Johnson's case was undermined by his reliance on statistics supplied by the Soviets, which Johnson did not bother to check. He wrote, "Some 50,000 priests live today in the Soviet Union. They are as free to vote at the polls as any other citizen." He painted a rosy picture of freedom and prosperity far removed from the truth. It was later discovered that Johnson did not write large sections of the book, which had been copied word for word from material supplied by the Soviets. Many critics, especially those who had first-hand experience of the communist regime, questioned Johnson's findings and described him as naïve.

Johnson was undaunted, however, and continued to proselytize on behalf of communism. He used his office as dean of the cathedral to take political aim at the United States and Britain, lambasting them for imperialism. Unsurprisingly, Johnson was frequently out of favor with the Archbishops of Canterbury under whom he served. He remained unswerving in his support for the Soviet Union and refused to condemn the Soviet Union when, in 1956, it sent tanks into Hungary to suppress the popular uprising.[22]

Rev. Hewlett Johnson at an award ceremony in Moscow in 1951, where he received the Stalin Peace Prize.

Johnson was an educated man with courteous manners and a generous nature, who believed that communist governments lifted working-class people out of poverty and raised standards of living for the ordinary working person. His many visits to communist countries, (all of which were paid for by his sponsors), convinced him that communism and Christianity were entirely compatible. While Johnson enjoyed the freedom to speak his mind on this subject, he overlooked the fact that this privilege was denied to the citizens of those countries whose governments he championed. At home, he lived more like a capitalist than a communist, investing in the stock market and owning eleven properties (while he and his family lived in the house provided by the church.)[23]

Johnson was a well-known clergyman who used his clerical and moral authority to preach a political gospel. It is a common practice nowadays, grounded in the notion that the church has a duty to speak out on moral issues, and that its voice should not be shackled by political constraints. In theory this makes sense, yet if a church aligns itself with a political party, as many do, it has effectively surrendered its authority to speak with an impartial voice, especially when it stifles criticism for fear of offending its political masters.

History provides several salutary examples of what happens when Church doctrine and theology become infiltrated by secular and progressive ideologies. In Nazi Germany, the German Christian movement (GDC) comprised over half a million members. The GDC merged Christianity with German nationalism, and in church services praised both Jesus and Hitler.[24] At the other end of the scale, Liberation Theology in the latter half of the twentieth century promoted the transformation of society into a Christian ideal through an alliance with Marxist ideology and practice, including educational indoctrination and an emphasis on armed struggle. How far it took Christianity from its core message is evidenced in the statement made by the African Conference of Churches in 1974, that "God has sanctified violence into a redemptive instrument for bringing into being a fuller human life."[25]

While many Christians approve of the Church's embrace of secular political movements, to the disinterested observer it can appear that the church's moral and spiritual authority is compromised. In his 1978 Reith lectures on Christianity and the World Order, the Rev. Edward Norman sees

> *...the politicization of Christianity as a symptom of its decay as an authentic religion. It is losing sight of its own rootedness in a spiritual tradition; its mind is progressively secularized; its expectations are prompted by worldly changes; and its moral idealism has forfeited transcendence.*[26]

Advocates of the politicization of the church claim that Jesus was "upending social structures that put people in the margins and justified oppression and exploitation," as I heard recently in a sermon. Certainly, Jesus came to change the way we think about ourselves and our relationship with God. But to say that Jesus wanted to "upend social structures" implies radical social realignment, which usually only occurs with political change or revolution. Activists often cite the Cleansing of the Temple (Mark 11:15-19) as evidence that Jesus favored violence as a way of reforming society. However, this is a misreading of the text, which describes not an incipient insurrection but Jesus responding to the sacrilege of buying and selling in the Temple, the holy place of God. If Jesus really meant to challenge the political rulers, why did he not enter the garrison of the Roman tribune and overturn the tables there?

Throughout his life, Jesus sought no political alliances. Presumably, there would have been opportunities for him to do so: with the Zealots, for example, who were committed to resistance against the Roman authorities. In fact, the message of the gospel is personal, not political: it is about a conversion of heart, not the overthrowing of the political order. (see Matthew 5:17; Mark 12:17).

Another problem for politicized clergy, especially those who hew to the left, is that, as Edward Norman observed,

> *Because Christian leaders tend to amateurism in the very professional business of political tactics…they make a simple, and generally innocent, conflation of Christian love of neighbor with the most hard-line Marxist devices to engineer radical social change. They represent the political rhetoric of Marxism as merely a succinct manner of expressing agreed moral truths about human society.*[27]

The Christian is called to a brave and self-sacrificial defense of the truths of the gospels. This is because truth, to a Christian, is something that exists in itself. The governor, Pontius Pilate, famously asked Jesus, "What is truth?" Pilate is used to disregarding truth when it is politically expedient to do so. The truth of Jesus' innocence, for example, Pilate disregards for political reasons; his primary role is to maintain public order, and he fears the reaction from the mob if he sets Jesus free. In effect, his question is really "What political power has truth?" as he proves that "truth" in itself has no power to save Jesus from execution.

The notion that truth has no political power should not bother the Christian at all. However, Marxists take a different view. For them, truth is subversive to political order. Hence the practice in communist countries of suppressing or manipulating the truth in order to promote the State agenda. The old Soviet joke, "The future is certain; it is only the past that is unpredictable," neatly captures this mindset. The Christians who fail to identify the threat posed by Marxism, contrary to all the evidence available, have loosed themselves from the moorings of truth and are adrift in a world of relativism that eventually leads to oblivion.

One needs to look no further than China today, where the encroachment of the communist state into every aspect of human life and endeavor is threatening the truth of the gospel message of Jesus Christ. In the West, the danger is less advanced but no less real. The decline in church attendance and Christian belief is a sign of the growing secularism of society. With the increase in secularism, especially where it is underpinned by an attachment to Marxist ideology, Christians can expect to be pushed further to the margins and treated with increasing intolerance.

The answer is for Christians to detach themselves from political ideology and hold fast to the gospel teachings. It may be that, sooner rather than later, Christian witness will become a test of faith, especially where persecution increases and Christians are accused of many failings and crimes. This is a path many Christians have taken before. It means going deeper into our faith and learning to cultivate an inner strength because the resources needed to overcome the pressures from outside will only come from a place of secure faith: of trust in God and adherence to the truth. What is at stake is nothing less than the integrity of the Church and the saving message of Christ in the world.

Notes

1.   Frederick Engels, "The Condition of England: A Review of Past and Present", by Thomas Carlyle, London 1843. (January 1844), *Deutsch-Französische Jahrbücher*, 1844. In: *Marx/Engels Selected Works*, Volume 3 (Progress Publishers, 1970), 446.

2.   Engels, 191.

3.   Daniel Peris, *Storming the Heavens* (New York: Cornell University Press, 1998), 85.

4.   Perris, 86.

5.   Frances X. Maier, "How Marxism Won the war of Ideas", *Wall Street Journal*, January 6, 2022. <https://www.wsj.com/articles/marxism-won-war-of-ideas-augusto-del-noce-gnosticism-Catholic-therapy-ai-mental-health-technology-11641483920> [accessed February 14, 2022].

6.   Augusto Del Noce, *The Problem of Atheism*, edited and translated by Carlo Lancellotti, (Montreal: McGill-Queens University Press, 2021), 312.

7.   Robert Conquest, *Reflections on a Ravaged Century*, (New York: W.W. Norton & Co., 2000), 94.

8.   Rod Dreyer, "Pope's 'Common Dreams' With Marxists Denies Persecution Nightmare" *The European Conservative*, January 11, 2024. <https://europeanconservative.com/articles/commentary/popes-marxist-dreams/> {accessed January 20, 2024}.

9.   Victoria Smolkin, *A Sacred Space is Never Empty* (Princeton: Princeton University Press, 2018), 47.

10.   Martin Amis, *Koba the Dread,* (New York: Hyperion Press, 2002), 75.

11.   Aldous Huxley, "Introduction" to *Erewhon*, by Samuel Butler. (New York: Limited Editions Club, 1934).

12.   David Pryce-Jones, "Eric Hobsbawm:Lying to the Credulous" in *Openings and Outings* (New York: Criterion, 2022), 154.

13.   Arthur Koestler, "The Initiates" in *The God That Failed*, ed. Richard Crossman (London: Hamilton, 1950), 23.

14.   Stephen Spender, "Worshipers From Afar" in *The God That Failed*, ed. Richard Crossman (London: Hamilton, 1950), 237.

15.   Ludmila Stern, *Western Intellectuals and the Soviet Union 1920-40* (Abingdon: Routledge, 2007), 16.

16.   Sean McMeekin, *To Overthrow the World* (NewYork: Basic Books, 2024), 225

17.   David Horowitz, *Radical Son (30th Anniversary Edition)* (New York: Bombadier Books, 2020), 112.

18.   Emma Goldman, *My Two Years in Russia* (St Petersburg: Red and Black, 2008), 83.

19.   Benedict Rogers, "Why China is Terrified of Christianity" *Unherd*, February 17, 2021. <https://unherd.com/2021/02/why-china-is-terrified-of-christianity/> {accessed February 14, 2022).

20.   John Butler, *The Red Dean* (London: Scala Publishers, 2011), 88.

21.   Butler, 89.

22.   Butler, 206.

23.   Butler, 191.

24.   David Chidester, *Christianity* (London: Allen Lane, 2000), 536.

25.   Edward Norman, *Christianity and the World Order* (Oxford: OUP, 1979), 60.

26.   Norman, 13.

27.   Norman, 18-19.

Chapter 10

Icons

I shall root you in the wood,
under the sun shall bake you bread
of beech mast, never let you forth
To the white desert, to the starving sand.
But we shall sit and speak around
one table, share one food, one earth.

From *Rublev*, by Rowan Williams[1]

What is an icon? Today, an icon is known primarily as the tiny image you click on to open up a web page, app, folder, or file. Its adjectival form, "iconic", is a salute to people or things which have become famous and significant. The Collins dictionary states that "if you describe something or someone as an icon, you mean that they are important as a symbol of a particular thing". The Argentine footballer Lionel Messi, famous for his skill on the ball, is an iconic figure. London double-decker buses are iconic. The Planar 3 turntable is a "Vinyl Icon", according to a company press statement. These days, it seems that anybody or anything can be an "icon".

However, its original meaning was much narrower. They were (and are) religious paintings found in Eastern Orthodox homes and churches. The word "icon" derives from the Greek *eikon*, which means "image". Icons were created as images of saints and of our Lord Jesus Christ.

Icons are important for the community of believers because they have spiritual value. In the Orthodox liturgy, icons have a specific theology and dogma. To Orthodox Christians, icons are not pictures; they are reminders of what is termed a *prototype*. The icon reminds us of God as the *prototype*, in whose image and likeness every human being is created. In the fourth century, St. Basil the Great explained that people should respect icons because "The honor given to the image passes over to the *Prototype*."[2]

There are rules laid down by the Church which govern the painting of icons. It might be useful here to draw a comparison with film. The filmmaker Werner Herzog described film as "not the art of scholars but of illiterates." These words echo St. John of Damascus, who wrote:

> *The image is a memorial, just what words are to a listening ear. What a book is to the literate, an image is to the illiterate. The image speaks to sight as words to hearing; through the mind, we enter into union with it.*[3]

Icons are theological—that is to say, they lead us to a deeper understanding and knowledge of God. The letter to the Hebrews states: "[Jesus] is the reflection of God's glory and the exact imprint of God's very being."(Hebrews 1:3) What is invisible cannot be depicted, but what is visible can be, since it is no longer the product of one's imagination but an actual, material reality. Having assumed fallen human nature, Christ restored in human beings the image of God in which we were created.

There are those who think that to make any holy image is to create an idol. Throughout history, there have been periods when icons have been destroyed and suppressed, from where we get the word "iconoclast". However, an image is not necessarily an idol. The function of the written word—the chief function of the Bible, is to lead us to a deeper understanding of God and ourselves. This is what icons do, using images instead of words. Icons act as mediators between God and humanity. What gives power to both is the action of the Holy Spirit in our hearts and minds, either in the reading of scripture or as we gaze meditatively at a holy icon.

Icons have a long history in the Church. The fourth-century church historian Eusebius noted: "I have seen a great many portraits of the Savior, of Peter and of Paul, which have been preserved up to our times." [4]Did icons or paintings of our Lord and the saints exist as early as the end of the first century AD? According to legend, the earliest icon was one of the Virgin Mary and Christ painted by the Evangelist Luke. Sadly, neither this icon nor any paintings as described by Eusebius have survived. It is certain that many have been lost as a result of iconoclasm.

When icons first appeared, their style bore the influence of the art of Egypt, Syria, and Asia Minor, particularly in the classical traditions of Alexandrian art, which had preserved Greek Hellenism in its purest form. We see these influences most markedly in the portraits from Pompeii.

The earliest surviving icon, which was discovered by chance in a small auction house in Avignon, France in 2003, dates from the sixth or seventh century AD. It is an icon of the Virgin and Child. The style is simple but undeniably powerful. Viewed simply as an art object, it is rudimentary and even primitive. However, to the person of prayer, the image has a spiritual power. An authentic icon draws you beyond the material world and into the world of angels and saints.

The icon is also the agent of dogma; its function is to communicate in visual terms the essential doctrines of Christianity: the Holy Trinity, the Incarnation, and the Saints. The iconographer— the one who creates icons—does not transmit his or her own idea, but "a description of what is contemplated." [5]

The Western notion of the "I" in art has no importance where icons are concerned—hence icons are not signed. When I visited the Tretyakov Gallery in Moscow in 2008 I made the simple mistake of asking a member of the gallery staff where the Rublev icons were located. She corrected me, "We do not speak of the icons as belonging to one artist or another."

A description of an icon painter is provided by the Orthodox theologian Leonid Ouspensky. He explains that

> *An iconographer must conform to an image consecrated by the Church, introducing no personal or emotional content, but placing all those who pray, before one and the same reality and leaving each person free to react to the extent of his or her possibilities and in accordance with his or her character, needs, circumstances and so forth. Moreover, just as a priest officiates according to his natural gifts and peculiarities, so an iconographer transmits an image according to his character, gifts, and technical proficiency.[6]*

Although icon painters are bound by rules and conventions, nevertheless there exists a small measure of stylistic freedom. Accordingly, this guarantees that each icon will be unique. Because iconographers make visual the mysteries of theology, they are not so much painters as writers, and the Orthodox Church, therefore, describes icons as having been "written" rather than "painted." Iconographers must be people of prayer, preferably ascetic in their lifestyle, and partaking fully in the sacramental life of the church. Being an icon "writer" makes religious and moral demands.

The Council of the Hundred Chapters decreed that the icon painter should be "meek, mild, and pious, not given to idle talk or to laughter, not quarrelsome or envious, not a thief or a murderer". The main demand was that the painter must show no independence, no "thinking for himself" in what he or she painted. However, we can also note that those icons we can attribute to particular "writers" evidence a refined level of technical and creative ability.

Theodosius the Hermit draws parallels between the iconographer and the priest. "For the priest, officiating with divine words prepares the Body of which we participate for the remission of sins; while the artist, instead of using words, draws and images a body and gives it life; and we venerate icons for the sake of their prototypes."[7]

There's that word *prototype* again. There are no icons of living persons. The icon represents a person in his or her transformed or deified state. It shows those who have gone over, whose corruptible human flesh has been replaced by the Incorruptible and eternal light of God. The subjects of icons are characterized by a certain spiritual reality: sober, grace-filled, and free of any exaltation. They are usually static images. The subject looks out at us directly, looking not so much into our eyes but into our souls.

In some icons, the proportions of the subject are exaggerated. In Orthodox tradition, this reflects the path to spiritual transformation as being that of asceticism, self-denial, and fasting. Therefore, hands and feet are sometimes thinner than they are in real life, while the facial features— the nose, eyes, and ears—are more oblong. All these and many other artistic techniques are employed to convey the spiritual change which happens to human flesh as a result of the asceticism and self-denial of the saint, along with the transforming impact made on them by the Holy Spirit.

Metropolitan Hilarion elaborates on this idea

> *The icon of a saint shows not so much a process as a result, not so much a way as a destination point, not so much a movement towards a goal but as a goal in itself. In an icon, we see someone who does not struggle with the passions but has overcome them, who does not seek the Heavenly Kingdom but who has already reached it.* [8]

In the West, we have been trained to see images in a certain way. Our primary lens is artistic, meaning that we tend to view an icon using the same mental apparatus as we would when admiring say, Van Gogh's Sunflowers. While it is natural to approach icons as art objects, their full value will only be realized once we are able to suspend our aesthetic judgment and allow the icon entry into our prayer life.

In personal prayer, the icon draws our intention and stills the mind. In the image of a saint, one recognizes both the human and divine as present. The icon acts as a bridge or window into eternity. Icons are also educational. For example, a believer who contemplates the icon of the Harrowing of Hell— Jesus' descent into Hell to set free those bound by Satan—is being instructed in the doctrine of the Church.

Icons also remind us that the saints pray with us. Anyone entering an Orthodox church or chapel for the first time will immediately be aware of a host of icons, on either side of the walls, along with a large iconostasis, or screen, separating the clergy from the congregation. Our worship combines heaven and earth in one unending hymn of praise.

The poem by Rowan Williams is inspired by the fifteenth-century icon of *The Hospitality of Abraham* or *Troitsa*, as it is also known. (Williams may have also seen the movie "Andrei Rublev", by Andrei Tarkovsky). This

Andrej Rublëv. *The Hospitality of Abraham*, c. 1411 or 1425-27, tempera on wood, 56 × 45 in., Old Katholikon of the Trinity Lavra, Sergiyev Posad, Russia.

particular icon is perhaps the most famous of all. It is one which, to borrow an expression from Walt Whitman, contains multitudes. There are multitudes of layers and meanings within its frame, but the overall impression is one of peace and harmony. It invites us forward and bids us join the three angels who are representative of the Holy Trinity. As in scripture, we find ourselves enveloped in the mystery of God's presence, expressed in terms of the divine relationship between the three persons of the Trinity.

Notes

1.   Rowan Williams, *The Poems of Rowan Williams*, (Oxford:Perpetua Press, 2002), 35.

2.   St. Theodore the Studite, *On the Holy Icons* (New York: SVS Press, 1997), 13.

3.   St. John Damascene, *On Holy Images* (London: Thomas Baker, 1898), 19.

4.   Elizabeth Zelensky and Lela Gilbert, *Windows to Heaven* (Grand Rapids: Brazos Press, 2005), 31.

5.   Leonid Ouspensky and Vladimir Lossky, *The Meaning of Icons* (Olten: Otto Walter, 1952), 43

6.   Ouspensky and Lossky, 44.

7.   Ouspensky and Lossky, 44.

8.   Metropolitan Hilarion, *Theology of Icon in the Orthodox Church*, Lecture at St. Vladimir's Seminary, 5 February 2011. <https://mospat.ru/en/news/56024/> Accessed December 9, 2024.

Chapter 11

A Black Hole

May 19, 2022

The shadow of a nearby black hole—named Sagittarius A*—has made the front pages of the newspapers. To refresh your memory, "black holes" form when a star goes supernova, shooting vast amounts of matter into space while folding in or collapsing upon itself. The image of the black hole's shadow looked like a blurry photo of three candles.

"Nearby" is a relative term when we are talking about space. Scientists reckon Sagittarius A* is between twenty-six and twenty-seven thousand light-years from Earth. I love the fact that the estimated distance is slightly inexact. Imagine a space capsule that sets off from Earth and then reaches the twenty-six thousand light-year mark, only for the astronauts to discover they have another thousand light-years yet to travel. As a reference, one light year equals six trillion miles.

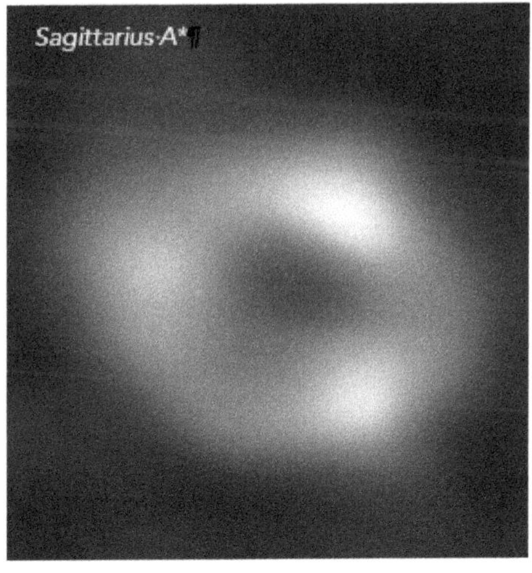

At four million times the size of our Sun, Sagittarius A* is considered by scientists to be a small black hole. Its closest neighbor, M87, is fifteen hundred times bigger. Thinking about these dimensions is almost impossible, given the scale and size of the universe. Our poor brains have enough difficulty figuring out things on earth, without the thought that, in the grand scheme of space, our planet is less than the size of an atom.

At the same time, it fills me with wonder. On our less than atom-sized planet, there is an almost endless variety of life. The conditions for life on Earth—atmosphere, temperature, etc.—appear almost miraculous in the context of space. It makes the argument for God's existence even more convincing, not less.

In the Book of Psalms, it is God who made the heavens and the earth, the "sea-monsters and all deeps…wild beasts and all cattle, creeping things and winged birds…and all peoples" (Psalm 148). God also created the universe and set us in the midst of it. While human beings think of themselves as whole and independent, in reality we are swirling around the universe like confetti in the wind. We are subject to change and movement, growth and decay, and to the mysterious energy of the Holy Spirit.

Believing that God is both the creator and sustainer of the universe helps me to understand my place in it. On the surface of things, it makes me feel insignificant and even meaningless. But if I go a little deeper, I can discover a spiritual world every bit as vast and deep as the physical world of space.

The door into this spiritual world is *prayer*, which opens the mind and heart to the presence of God. To pray is like beginning a voyage of discovery. Prayer (and worship) are the building blocks for the spiritual universe into which God calls us. Unlike the physical world of space, God is not distant like a black hole. God sets in motion the movement of the world and the universe in which planets, galaxies, and black holes share space with angels, demons, and saints.

If you are used to keeping your eyes fixed on the ground, now might be the time to lift them heavenwards. You will be pleasantly surprised. The spiritual realm is closer than you think.

Chapter 12

Growing old

May 12, 2022

The world's oldest person, Kane Tanaka, died last week in Fukuoka in southern Japan. According to the hospital spokesman, the cause of death was old age. She was 119 years old.

How do you live as long as 119 years? Mrs Tanaka had her own advice: "Don't give up and say there's no point. Live with all your heart." Centenarians are always asked about the secret to a long life. One extolls the benefits of a nightly glass of brandy. Others talk about the importance of keeping a positive attitude. My favorite comment is from a 100-year-old man who drank and smoked all his life: "If I knew I was going to live this long, I would have taken better care of myself."

Is there a good reason for living so long? In traditional societies, living to a ripe old age is considered beneficial, since the "elders", as they are known, contribute to society out of their store of wisdom and experience. However, not all old people are wise.

The Bible presents some colorful examples of not-so-wise elders. In the first book of Kings, King Solomon began as a wise young king but became less so the older he got. In the first chapter of the gospel of Luke, the elderly priest Zechariah is visited by the angel Gabriel. The angel brings tidings that Zechariah's wife Elizabeth will conceive and bear a son. Had he been wise, Zechariah would have accepted the news with gracious silence. Instead, he questioned how Elizabeth could bear a son in her old age. For his lack of discretion, God struck Zechariah mute (although not forever).

William Blake, *The Angel Appearing to Zacharias*, c. 1799 - 1800, pen and black ink, tempera, and glue size on canvas, 10 1/2 × 15 in. (26.7 x 38.1 cm), The Metropolitan Museum of Art, New York.

One of the aspects of old age is the accumulation of memories. The older you get, the more memories you accrue. These personal memories are like chapters in a manuscript for an autobiography. However, memories are susceptible to being rewritten over the years. If I recall a shared event from years ago with my children, they usually remember it differently from me. I shake my head when I hear some of the things I'm supposed to have said. The subconscious editing of past events sometimes serves to put you in a more favorable light than you deserve. Memory is subject to vanity.

Unlike the centenarians mentioned above, I don't have a clear philosophy about growing old, but I have kept in mind what others have said or done. As a creative artist, the jazz trumpeter Miles Davis had an attitude of always looking forward rather than back. I saw him play late in his career, and he was still trying out new things and hewing his own creative path, rather than playing "hits" or trying to please the crowd. Miles' attitude could be rather prickly. After one solo, the audience was insufficiently appreciative. Miles glowered at us.

The wisdom of the poet T. S. Eliot also inspires me. "Old men ought to be explorers," he wrote in his poem East Coker. This maxim applies whether you are male or female. There is always something new to learn, or a new path to take, or a new ministry to discover.

One of the challenges of growing old is learning to cope with the knocks and tragedies that accumulate over time. When a spouse, partner, or close friend dies, they leave a gap that no one else can fill. It is hard to outlive a loved one. For the survivor, the mantle of grief can be worn for the rest of their life. Finding a new life begins with giving one's heart to God and asking for strength. In Christ, there is hope. As Eliot says, we can continue to explore. Creativity can also be a healing balm.

"Don't give up and say there's no point. Live with all your heart." Kane Tanaka's simple philosophy of life encapsulates the daily wrestle to find meaning and the best way of achieving it. Life can be hard, and it is easy to become disheartened. God is our help in times of need, and his spirit guides us along the way. Our teacher in life is Jesus Christ, who lived with all his heart and gave up his own life for the sake of many. The lives of the saints—those who have followed Jesus—can be inspiring to us. The aim of life is not to live 119 or 219 years but to live well in the years you have. A long life can be a blessing, especially if you have the right attitude.

Chapter 13

The Queen is Dead

September 8, 2022

Today the whole world received the news of the death of Queen Elizabeth II. She was 96 years old and had reigned for over 70 years. Her final public duty occurred two days earlier when she met with and formally appointed Liz Truss as the new Prime Minister of the United Kingdom. Truss was the last prime minister to speak with her, the first having been Winston Churchill.

It's a cliché to say that the Queen's death marks the end of an era, but it is certainly true. She did not have political power and her role was essentially ceremonial. Yet her influence was great, from her weekly meetings with prime ministers to her own life of public duty and service.

I grew up during her reign, seeing her on coins and banknotes every day. Until the 1970s, the feature movie in cinemas wouldn't begin until the national anthem had played. As the curtain drew back, the audience would stand respectfully and view an old color film of the royal family sitting together.

My mother felt an affinity for the Queen because both women had four children, born more or less at the same time. I can also claim a distant (six generations removed) kinship with the Queen: our family is related by virtue of our shared Scottish ancestry—the Queen Mother was a Scot.

Elizabeth Alexandra Mary, Elizabeth II, by the Grace of God, of the United Kingdom of Great Britain and Northern Ireland and of her other realms and territories Queen, Head of the Commonwealth, Defender of the Faith (April 21, 1926, London, England - September 8, 2022, Balmoral Castle, Aberdeenshire, Scotland).

The Queen lived a long life of service to God and country. However, during the recent media coverage of the Platinum Jubilee celebration, I noticed that the announcers omitted any mention of the Queen's Christian faith. Perhaps this reflects the fact that some commentators are no longer comfortable with the idea that religious faith can be central or even beneficial to a person's life.

It was the Queen's faith that gave her the strength to carry out the role to which she was born. At her coronation—a service built around the liturgy of Holy Communion—she vowed to protect the Church of England and preserve its bishops and clergy. Hence, one of her titles was "Defender of the Faith."

Every Christmas Day, the Queen made a speech that, since 1957, has been broadcast on television. She always spoke openly about her Christian faith and how it gave her the strength to serve others. On Christmas Day in 1952, before her coronation, she humbly asked her subjects,

> Whatever your religion may be, to pray for me on that day—to pray that God may give me wisdom and strength to carry out the solemn promises I shall be making, and that I may faithfully serve Him and you, all the days of my life.

In her 1957 broadcast she gave a warning about those who "would have religion thrown aside, morality in personal and public life made meaningless, honesty counted as foolishness and self-interest set up in place of self-restraint." She followed with words that speak to us today.

> Today we need a special kind of courage, not the kind needed in battle but a kind which makes us stand up for everything that we know is right, everything that is true and honest. We need the kind of courage that can withstand the subtle corruption of the cynics so that we can show the world that we are not afraid of the future. It has always been easy to hate and destroy. To build and to cherish is much more difficult.

In our divisive and increasingly secular age, it is good to be reminded of the need to hold fast to the truth, to have hope for the future, and to count ourselves among hope's builders, no matter how difficult. The Queen's speech is evidence of God's mind in her own thinking, and an abiding message for our time.

Well done, good and faithful servant!

Chapter 14

Politics

February 3, 2024

We were about to begin Morning Prayer when my wife noticed them. Two stink bugs five feet apart on the moldings above the living room window. They must have entered our house through a secret entrance. We regularly evict such intruders or consign them to a watery grave, yet they persist in coming inside and sharing our space.

We watched as the bugs started their slow march toward one another. It was fascinating to observe them, as they slowly but deliberately headed for a showdown. I said there should be a crescendo of orchestral music to accompany the impending encounter. Was it two lovers meeting, or two adversaries about to join in mortal combat? The moment came, when at last the two stink bugs met, face to face. They appeared to kiss, and then one climbed over the other and each carried on their respective way.

It is an election year, and the two stick bugs reminded me of our two probable presidential candidates, Mr. Biden and Mr. Trump. I don't know why they should, but they do. If you are reading this and think I am being disrespectful, I apologize. Usually I avoid commenting on political matters, but with the general election less than nine months away, I am inspired by the stink bugs to share my two cents early.

It's no secret that the country is polarized and that dialogue between supporters of our respective political parties is almost impossible. I scratch my head and wonder why. The old slogan, now discredited, "My country, right or wrong", has been replaced by "My party, right or wrong." People take politics personally, but I am not sure that that is always a good thing.

Sometimes churches take sides. This is a mistake, I believe, and often results in a hijacking of the gospel to feed a political vanity. Because I want the Church of the Messiah to be a spiritual home for Democrats and Republicans alike, I will avoid the temptation to speak out or advocate for one side over another. I have seen what damage "political" priests do to a congregation, in creating division and misrepresenting Jesus' message.

There is another reason why the church should remain neutral. Christians as a group are called to model a different type of living. If society is divided, Christians can demonstrate by their words and actions what a united society looks like. We do this not by appealing to our partisan instincts, but by being true to our promises to Christ. Christians seek peace and reconciliation for the benefit of the whole community. By avoiding political arguments, we can offer an oasis of godly peace among the clamor of voices that will dominate our lives over the next nine months.

In this regard, consider this a test of faith. Our identity as Christians matters more than our identity as political creatures. There is a good reason why Jesus did not confront Pontius Pilate. The political will is a will to power, whereas Christ taught and lived a gospel of humility. The one who had ultimate power "did not regard equality with God as something to be exploited, but emptied himself, taking the form of a slave" (Philippians 2:6-7).

Set a course this year that will avoid the seductive draw of politics, with its tendency to create demons of our neighbors and set us against one another. There's a better life for us to show others—the way of Christ, the reconciler and savior of souls.

Chapter 15

Plugging In

My ten-year-old car died and went to car heaven. Actually, I took it to the dealer for repairs and he called me back saying, "I hate having to make these calls…" It turns out the transmission needed replacing. He apologized for the breakdown and explained that the cost of repairs exceeded the total value of the car. So I sold it back to the dealer for a pittance. The car had 115,000 miles on the clock.

My wife and I then spent a month figuring out what car we would get to replace it. In the end, we plumped for an electric vehicle, a Hyundai Ioniq6. We road-tested a Tesla Model 3, which was fun, but we found the ride too bumpy. The Tesla has a minimalist ethic, and nearly everything is accessed via a touch screen. The Ioniq6, on the other hand, has a smoother ride and retro buttons and dials. It also looks fantastic.

We're leasing it, which allowed the dealer to use a Federal tax credit to reduce the price by $7,500. The state of Delaware also gave us $2,500. The icing on the cake is free public charging for two years, so long as you charge at Electrify America. They have several charging stations in Pennsylvania, but only one in Delaware.

The person who imagines a future where everyone drives electric vehicles has probably never owned one. I love mine, but when it comes to charging, you plug in and spend up to thirty minutes at the charging station. The other day, as I was waiting my turn, I noticed that one of the charging stations had been occupied for over 50 minutes. Obviously, going to a charger is not as convenient as going to a gas station.

At a gas station, you fill up and go. It takes less than five minutes. EV owners are different. After plugging in, you might get out of your car and walk around and talk to another EV owner. I've had some good conversations this way. One person had an Ioniq6 like me, and both of us said it was the only other one they had ever seen. It felt like belonging to an exclusive club.

Most EV owners sit in their cars when charging. As it happens, the thirty-minute period is about the same time as it takes to say the office of Morning Prayer. Sometimes, that is what I do. I use the Church of England app, which provides Morning and Evening Prayer. It includes all the Scripture readings and prayers for each day.

A parishioner regretted not making enough time for prayer. My advice was that they should buy an electric car. Failing that, I said that they should set aside thirty minutes each day to say the "daily office". It's a holy discipline that has been observed in the Church for hundreds of years. It will broaden your knowledge of Scripture and help to keep you close to God. When you pray, your prayers are joined with the prayers of the whole company of heaven. God takes our prayers and uses them to heal and bless the world.

Sometimes being a Christian feels like belonging to an exclusive club although, as Archbishop Temple said, "The Church exists primarily for the sake of those who are still outside it." That means the church is for everyone. When we pray it is like being plugged into a spiritual network. It costs nothing too—only your time and commitment.

Chapter 16

Seven Years in Tibet

Seven Years in Tibet is a movie based on the 1952 memoir of Austrian mountain climber Heinrich Harrer. In 1939 Harrer went to India with a group of mountaineers to attempt an ascent of "Nanga Parbat", the ninth-highest mountain on earth. When World War II broke out, Harrer and the group were arrested by the British authorities and interned in a POW camp. The group escaped from the camp and Harrer and his fellow mountaineer Peter Aufschnaiter found refuge in the neighboring country of Tibet.

Tibet was then a country which time seemed to have passed by. Its culture and traditions were steeped in Buddhism. The dream-like landscape of Tibet—rocky plains and valleys set against a backdrop of snowcapped Himalayan Mountains—had a dislocating effect on the two escapees. Gradually they became immersed in the rituals and customs of this ancient kingdom.

Harrer met the spiritual and political leader of Tibet, His Holiness the 14th Dalai Lama. At that time, the Dalai Lama was a boy monk, the reincarnation of the 13th Dalai Lama. The Austrian and the young Tibetan quickly became friends. Harrer had to answer an endless stream of questions about the outside world from the curious boy monk. Unafraid of modern technology, the Dalai Lama even asked Harrer to build a cinema in the ancient capital of Lhasa.

His Holiness the Fourtenth Dalai Lama. Photo: Brian Beresford

Tibet's autonomous rule was brought to an end when China invaded the country in 1950. This is an often overlooked chapter in the history of twentieth-century crimes. Although the movie shows the massacre of the ill-equipped Tibetan forces by battle-hardened veterans of the Red Army, it does not dwell on the consequences of the invasion. However, in the final credits, it does note the death of over a million Tibetans at the hands of the Chinese, along with the desecration and vandalism of Tibetan Buddhist temples and homes.

Much of this story was already familiar to me. I had heard it from my brother Brian, who lived in India in the 1970s, who in turn had heard it from the Tibetan exiles whom Brian had met. It would take several chapters to describe my brother's story. Brian began his career as a studio photographer in Auckland, New Zealand. In the early 1970s, he and his wife embarked on a journey across Asia, ending up in the town of Dharamsala, Northern India, where for seven years they lived and raised two children.

My brother's meeting with the Dalai Lama was to change his life. Brian studied at the Library of Tibetan Works and Archives, where he taught himself to read and write Tibetan. He translated many ancient Tibetan scrolls into English—the most well-known is *Advice from a Spiritual Friend*. He gave me a copy of the book in 1978, which was the year I went with my parents and younger sister to visit him and his wife. Watching the movie brought back memories of that visit.

Himalayan Pilgrim, Photo: Brian Beresford

From Dharamsala, Brian set out alone to visit Persia (as it was then) and Afghanistan, taking numerous photographs. When the family moved to London in 1980, Brian set up a business in New Oxford Street. Many years later he held a public exhibition in London of his remarkable photographs; I remember him working through the night, hanging every photo hours before the exhibition opened.

In the years before his death, Brian led groups of pilgrims annually into Tibet. Being a fluent speaker of Tibetan was an asset, along with a knowledge of the local geography and customs. When Brian died of a virus in 1997, the Dalai Lama personally sent a Tibetan scarf to the family, to be wrapped around the urn containing Brian's ashes. His family later traveled to India, where some of the ashes were scattered. It was somehow fitting that he was returned in this way to the place of his spiritual rebirth.

One day I would like to meet His Holiness the Dalai Lama and ask him about my brother. Maybe he could explain to me why two men from the same family traveled such a long way along different spiritual paths. (Our family has no history of priests, pastors, or lamas.)

I may not get the chance—the Dalai Lama is 89 years old. For all of his life, he has been a shining example of humility, joy, and compassion. He continues to vex the Chinese communists, who make themselves look foolish by their continual and exaggerated personal attacks on him. His answer is the Buddhist way of gentleness, peace, and reconciliation, which confounds those who reject the transcendent dimension of human life.

Brian deeply admired and loved this humble leader of Tibet. While the advanced practices of Buddhism require much discipline and study, its essential wisdom can be easily conveyed. In the beginning of an interview with the BBC's Jeremy Paxman in 1999, the Dalai Lama was described by Paxman as a living God and then asked how he would like to be addressed. The Dalai Lama considered for a moment, and then replied: "simple human brother."

Chapter 17

The Patriarch

In the book of Genesis, God established a covenant with Abraham to make him the ancestor "of a multitude of nations" (Genesis 17:5). God promised to be with Abraham's descendants forever, "throughout the generations." This passage came to mind in 2024 as my wife and I travelled to Petaluma, California for my father-in-law's ninety-fifth birthday party.

From north, south, and east all came to join the celebration. Several generations were present, including one yet to be born, expected in June. There were dinners on Friday and Saturday evenings, as well as lunch and dinner on Sunday. One of the newest family members—a fiancé of one of the family—remarked that the whole event felt like an Irish wedding (he used to live in Dublin) and that, of course, meant plenty of socializing.

On Sunday the reception hall was made ready for my father-in-law and his wife. The tables were laid and the food prepared. On the wall there was a large banner hung, which read, "95: More damn fun!" When the honored guests arrived, they were warmly greeted with applause. As the applause died down, my father-in-law spoke: "I thank you all for coming to celebrate my ninety-fifth birthday. I wasn't sure I was going to make it to this day. I could go at any time." Here he paused, before saying, "But then, so could all of you!" After a brief moment of stunned silence, the whole room erupted into laughter. It was the perfect, bitter-sweet beginning to the party.

Cesare Fantetti (after Raphael), *Promise to Abraham* (*Promessa per Abramo)*, c. 1841, embossed steel etching, 8 21/32 × 10 13/64 in. (220 x 259 cm).

I doubt my father-in-law will live as long as Abraham, who died at 175. Long after we have all passed away, it is the stories and example of our lives that will endure. I heard plenty of stories over those three days, as people recounted their joys and tragedies, and shared current concerns for one another. One particularly moving story was told by a sixty-five-year-old friend of the family. He recounted how, as a boy and an outsider, he had been warmly welcomed into the family as one of their own.

Of course, every family has its share of good stories and horror stories. However, over those three days everyone who was present believed that belonging to a family mattered. Bound together by love, the family was continuing to unfold across the generations, as new members arrived and found their place in the story.

Another kind of family to which we belong is the Church. God "destined us for adoption as his children through Jesus Christ" (Ephesians 1:5). Those who sit beside us in church are our brothers and sisters in Christ. We call God "our Father" and Jesus his son. As Christians, we do not exist in an atomized reality apart from one another. We are all related through baptism.

God's blessing for Abraham and his descendants is like a single thread woven into the good and bad stories of their lives. Likewise, in the messy reality of our own lives, the faithfulness of God abides. From God we learn the importance of keeping family ties alive, and seeing ourselves as belonging to something far greater than ourselves.

Chapter 18

The Lord is My Pilot

While sorting through some papers, I came across a memoir from my friend Chris, who died in 2020. The memoir is called Deep Waters and Far Away Places: The Vague Recollections of a Merchant Mariner. The title captures something of Chris's self-deprecatory nature and sense of humor.

In his early adult life, Chris was an apprentice in the Merchant Navy, and the memoir recounts his various experiences and escapades from 1956 to 1962, when he was employed by the British India Steam Navigation Company, or "B.I." for short. The company's name harkens back to a different time, when the sun was setting on the British Empire.

The memoir has value as a family record. At the time, few people journeyed abroad to the extent we do now, and international travel was the preserve of the well-off. However, for a ship's crew, it was a different story. Merchant mariners could sail the world and get paid for it, provided they did their jobs and looked after the passengers.

Much of a merchant mariner's life is mundane. Lifeboat drills, which involve launching and retrieving lifeboats, are common. There is cargo to load and unload. If you didn't get on with the skipper, tough luck. On one ship, Chris got completely drenched when the skipper took a dislike to him and made him stand on the bridge during a storm.

The M.V. "Chantala," built in 1950.

On shore, the crew could find other things to do. In Sydney, Chris met an Australian girl and courted her for a while. However, there was not enough time for the relationship to blossom. Later, he would meet his future wife Sandy in the ship's dispensary. Although life at sea could be tedious, there were also moments of transcendence. In the memoir, there is this passage where the author waxes lyrical.

> *There were, of course, many fine days of light airs, calm seas and gentle swells, when the early movement of air was created by the ship's progress through the breathless air…the only sounds were the tumbling waters of the bow wave, and the turbulence of the foaming wake training in a straight silvery ribbon towards the horizon behind us. These were the days and nights of cloudless skies when blazing sun gave way to the blackest backdrop to a billion sparkling galaxies, and a man would gaze up at the heavens and wonder if the human race could really be alone in the universe.*

Chris acknowledged the importance of the Mission to Seamen, a Christian organization dedicated to offering support, friendship and hospitality to seamen who were a long way from home. He describes the chaplains and volunteers at the various ports of call as his "first encounters with real Christians doing the Lord's work in a practical and meaningful way."

When I met Chris, his seafaring days were behind him, and I acted as a kind of chaplain to him at a time when his spirits were low. We formed a friendship and he was kind enough to send me his memoir.

He ends his memoir with the twenty-third psalm, in a version by Captain John Roberts, written in 1874. For those who venture out to sea—if we go back in time, this includes the disciples—the substitution of "pilot" for "shepherd" would have made perfect sense. Throughout his life Chris recognized the hand of Almighty God guiding him and keeping him safe from harm. He came to see where God had blessed him and how, in times of darkness, God had sent out a lifeline to him.

The Lord is my Pilot,
I shall not drift.
He lighteth me across the dark waters;
He steereth me in deep channels;
He keepeth my log.
He guideth me by the Star of Holiness for His Name's sake.
Yea, though I sail mid the thunders and tempests of life,
I will dread no danger, for Thou art with me;
Thy love and Thy care, they shelter me.
Thou preparest a harbor before me in the homeland of Eternity.
Thou anointest the waves with oil.
My ship rideth calmly.
Surely sunlight and starlight shall favor me on the voyage I take,
and I will rest in the port of my God for ever.

Chapter 19

Colin

I often find myself remembering an old friend or acquaintance whom I may not have seen or spoken to for years. In a daydream their face unexpectedly appears, and I begin to recall things they said or did. Sometimes the remembrance of them is triggered by a place, or a dream, or a passage of music, although equally there may be no obvious reason for their re-emergence from my subconscious mind.

It happened again this week. The person I remembered was Colin, whom I first met over forty years ago. He was artistic director for a theater company in Brighton, England, where I also worked for a time when I was in my twenties. In those days, a theater production would open on a Thursday evening and run for ten days, with the final performance on Saturday night. Then we would throw a party to celebrate the end of the season. The following day, the hungover theater crew would make their way back to the theater, dismantle the old set and begin erecting the new one.

With only a few days to turn things around, we were always under pressure. Colin oversaw the rehearsals with the actors as well as helping to build the new set. We had a good camaraderie, and after a day's work we would usually walk a short distance up the hill to the Battle of Trafalgar pub, (nicknamed the Botty) for a few beers.

The work didn't pay well. Eventually I left the theater and got myself a full time job. I lost touch with Colin, who continued as artistic director. Later, the theater closed and then re-opened under new management.

I saw Colin again many years later. He turned up at the Anglo-Catholic church where I worshiped. He was no longer working in the theater. His marriage had ended and he was an alcoholic. However, he was still the same Colin, who could confidently criticize the shortcomings of the Eucharistic celebration from an aesthetic and dramatic point of view. He would say, "if you're going to do it, then do it properly!" Overall, he enjoyed the high church worship, with its incense and long processions.

A year later he stopped coming to church. I don't know the exact reason. I lost touch with him for the second time. Our paths crossed again a few years later, this time in different circumstances. He was sitting in a bar, not far from where I lived. He was cheerful but looking worse for wear. Unlike some drunks, who become angry or belligerent, Colin's drinking made him amiable and gregarious.

I met him at a time when my own life was in crisis. I was off sick from work, due to stress—the new boss was making my life hell. Seeing Colin in the bar, I sat down with him and he ordered a bottle of wine. We talked about old times and the church. Then we ordered another bottle. I shared with him my tale of woe. He listened sympathetically, and probably gave advice, although I can no longer remember it. We both got very drunk that evening, but the combination of alcohol and Colin's companionship helped to take the sharp edges off my troubles.

One thing I remember from that evening was another person coming into the bar and joining us. He was a friend of Colin's. When Colin left us alone for a minute or two, the man told me that Colin had helped him when his own life was in crisis. Colin had been the friend he needed at the right time. Later I discovered that Colin had befriended a number of people in this way, and had dispensed advice and sympathy, along with liberal quantities of red wine.

Colin died the following year. I used to admire his talent and ability as a theater director, which was his true vocation. Later, when alcohol had taken that from him, he struggled to get by. By the end of his life, he only had himself left, but still had the heart to love and to give. Whether deliberately or not, he found a ministry to serve others.

Colin was a kind of saint—not a picture postcard one, but more of the down-to-earth kind. When I remember him, my feeling is one of gratitude. He helped me to get a little perspective on my own problems at a critical time in my life. I soon found a new job and a new direction. I learned that life goes on, as it does for Colin, who I pray now shares a heavenly home with the faithful departed in God's kingdom.

Chapter 20

Resurrection

In 2011 I served as an assistant chaplain at Ford Prison in the south of England. HMP Ford is a category D open prison, housing offenders with less than two years remaining on their sentence. While not exactly a holiday camp, it doesn't feel like a regular prison. During the day, prisoners are free to walk the grounds and at weekends some are given permission to leave and stay with family and friends. The prison has a farm shop which sells produce from the prison farm. Some offenders have paid jobs inside the prison. The prison's operation is designed to prepare inmates for life on the outside.

I have fond memories of the place. It was in the prison chapel that I presided at my first Easter Day Eucharist. The congregation had no difficulty in identifying with Jesus Christ who, like them, had been arrested, tried and convicted. Our all-male assembly had a different vibe to a regular congregation, where women usually outnumber the men. It changed the way I preached too; my sermons became shorter and more "to the point".

The chapel has a piano which was played during worship. The prisoners did a decent job of singing the hymns, although they were not going to win any competitions. At the altar I was assisted by the main prison chaplain. The readings were done by another clergyman who happened to be serving time for fraud. At the end of the service, the clergy and inmates all enjoyed tea and biscuits—some Anglican traditions never change.

Outside of regular worship times, the chapel remained open for anyone who wanted to pray. Not many did. The piano was available however, and

Entrance to HMP Ford

any offender with musical ability could come in and play. One of these was Graham Stubbs, or "Stubbsy", as the other prisoners called him. I never found out what he was in for; usually an offender would tell me, but if they didn't, I never asked.

Stubbsy would come into the chapel and play most days. He specialized in Chopin's Nocturnes. Now, anyone who knows anything about music will tell you how difficult it is play Chopin, not only in technique but in getting the right feeling. I have heard the Nocturnes played many times by many different pianists and the best, in my opinion, was Arthur Rubinstein. When Graham Stubbs played, it was like hearing Rubinstein play.

One of the most remarkable things about his playing was that he had learned all the pieces by ear. He told me that he hoped to make his living as a musician when he was released. Discovering his musical talent in prison had given him a new direction and identity. This became crystal clear to me when he asked me not to call him by his nickname, Stubbsy, but by his real name, Graham Stubbs. The tomb of prison had become a chrysalis wherein the old lag Stubbsy was being transformed into the new person, the musician Graham Stubbs.

The unfolding of Graham's musical talent is a story about resurrection. In Eastertide we think of Jesus Christ rising to new life, but resurrection is also about turning human lives from dead ends into living dreams. Resurrection gives us the inspiration to re-imagine our lives; as George Eliot once wrote, "it is never too late to be what you might have been." Resurrection can trigger that change because in its light we are no longer afraid but confident in the power of God to set us free.

I never found out if Graham achieved his ambition. Even if he didn't, he knew there was something more he could offer the world. I admired him for his determination to prove the doubters and naysayers wrong. In prison he had discovered a God-given talent that pointed in an entirely different direction to the one which had led him there.

Chapter 21

Peace

In the middle of the liturgy of the Holy Eucharist, the focus of attention shifts from the lectern, pulpit, and presider to the congregation. At that point, everyone in church is invited to exchange "the Peace". Worshippers turn toward one another and offer a handshake, a nod, or an embrace while saying "The Peace of the Lord be with you."

The Episcopal Dictionary defines Peace as "a sign of reconciliation, love, and renewed relationships in the Christian community."

Peace as a *liturgical* action (not as an opportunity for chit-chat) has its origin in the resurrection appearances of Jesus Christ, who greets his disciples with the words, "Peace be with you". (John 20:19). In this context, Peace is the promise of God's abiding and irrevocable blessing.

The Peace of God is not of the same order as the peace which human beings make for themselves. Peace on human terms is the result of the end of conflict or war. When the fighting between two enemies ceases, the work of peace begins. This is a work of rebuilding, both literally and psychologically. It is a work freighted with hope and fear. President Hoover remarked that "Peace is not made at the council tables, or by treaties, but in the hearts of men".

Henri Nouwen, (January 24, 1932 – September 21, 1996), professor of Divinity at Harvard College, Cambridge, Massachusetts.

Unlike human peace, which requires an absence of war, God's peace can be received at any time. It is a profound reassurance which is aimed at the human heart. If one were to search for a simple definition of God's Peace, these words of Julian of Norwich would suffice: "All shall be well, and all shall be well, and all manner of things shall be well."

All was not well with the Roman Catholic priest Henri Nouwen, who was a professor of Divinity at Harvard College, Cambridge, Massachusetts in the 1980s. Here he had established a reputation as a teacher, spiritual guide, and esteemed author of spiritual books. He was a highly respected member of the faculty, and people sought his advice and spiritual direction. On the surface, it appeared that he had achieved all of his life's ambitions and more. But the highly competitive atmosphere at Harvard was, in his words, "so marked by rivalry and competition, so pervaded with compulsion and obsession, so spotted with moments of suspicion, jealousy, resentment, and revenge,"[1] that Nouwen sought to escape.

He asked himself the question, "Is this really what I want to do for the rest of my life?" Nouwen made the decision to quit academic life. He then spent nine months at the L'Arche community in France. From there, he traveled to Toronto, where he joined a community near Toronto called "Daybreak"—a "family" comprising ten people, six of whom had intellectual disabilities. The community made it their mission to live by the beatitudes of Jesus Christ.

In "Daybreak", Nouwen found employment of a radically different kind: he was given the task of caring for one of the disabled persons there, a man named Adam. Nouwen described his friend:

> *Adam is a 25-year-old man who cannot speak, cannot dress or undress himself, cannot walk alone, and cannot eat without much help. He does not cry or laugh. Only occasionally does he make eye contact. His back is distorted. His arm and leg movements are twisted. He suffers from severe epilepsy and, despite heavy medication, sees few days without grand-mal seizures. Sometimes, as he grows suddenly rigid, he utters a howling groan. On a few occasions I've seen one big tear roll down his cheek.*

> *It takes me about an hour and a half to wake Adam up, give him his medication, carry him into his bath, wash him, shave him, clean his teeth, dress him, walk him to the kitchen, give him his breakfast, put him in his wheelchair and bring him to the place where he spends most of the day with therapeutic exercises.*[2]

This demanding daily routine was a severe test for the former academic. Most people would have given up. For Nouwen, however, the experience was a revelation. He writes, "As my fears gradually lessened, a love emerged in me so full of tender affection that most of my other tasks seemed boring and superficial compared with the hours spent with Adam. Out of his broken body and broken mind emerged a most beautiful human being, offering me a greater gift that I would ever offer him". What Adam gave Nouwen was the gift of peace.

He says, "Adam's peace, while rooted more in being than in doing, and more in the heart than in the mind, is a peace that calls forth community…Adam in his total vulnerability calls us together as a family."[3]

At Harvard, Nouwen had experienced prestige, fortune, and fame, but also the shallow rivalry and corrosive pettiness of the academic world. It drove him to seek a new and better life. In fact, what Nouwen had been longing for was *peace*: a genuine experience of God's peace which he found in a relationship with another person. In imitation of Christ, Nouwen found peace in self-giving love.

Of course, one cannot give love endlessly without receiving love in return. The revelation for Nouwen was that Adam, whether consciously or not, was able to return the love he received. Nouwen said, "It is I, not Adam, who gets the main benefit from our friendship."

When the resurrected Jesus stood before the disciples and said, "Peace be with you", he was blessing them as a community of the faithful. Until they received the peace, the disciples were in fear for their lives and meeting behind locked doors. The peace that Jesus bestowed gave them the confidence to set aside their fears and break out of their self-contained prison. This was Jesus' intention, that they would take the risk of creating communities of peace reaching beyond their own circle.

In the same way, Nouwen was trapped within the walls of academia. While providing him with status and recognition, he needed a real experience of love to find fulfillment. Unwilling to break his priestly vows and seek companionship in a sexual relationship, Nouwen found, almost by accident, the relationship that allowed his soul to be healed. Away from the trappings of fame and prestige, he found peace in a loving and giving human relationship. It was Adam, Nouwen wrote, who taught him that "what makes us human is not our mind but our heart, not our ability to think but our ability to love."

Notes

1.   Henri Nouwen, "Adam's Place" in *Shadow and Light*, Eds. Darryl Tippens, Stephen Weathers, Jack Welch (Abilene: A.C.U. Press, 1997), 67.

2.   Nouwen, 66.

3.   Nouwen, 68.

Chapter 22

Sanctifying Time

I recently attended a Church Pension Fund conference held for those approaching retirement. As you would expect, there were presentations about pensions and Medicare and how to make the most of your savings. There was also time to discuss the spiritual and psychological sides of retirement. The foremost question was "How to keep a work/life balance and stay healthy".

For the committed clergyperson, leading a church can be an all-consuming passion. Clergy are expected to be on duty 24/7 and prepared to deal with a variety of pastoral challenges. To make time for rest and recreation, I suggested that clergy needed to physically remove themselves from the church environment at least once a week.

One attendee had another idea. She showed us her old-fashioned flip phone. She said, "I only use this to take phone calls." No texts, email, or the internet. If someone needed to contact her urgently, all they had to do was dial the number and she would answer. The idea that a phone was to be used exclusively for phone calls—its original purpose—sounded strangely liberating.

But what about those who don't? For such people - who will soon be *everyone* - the idea of using a smartphone only for conversation would seem as strange as playing tennis with a wooden racquet or writing letters by hand. Smartphones are ubiquitous; they are our constant companions, providing us with access to the world through texts, calls, and the Internet.

However, perhaps the lady with a flip phone had a point. Could the hours of online activity be spent more profitably? Was all of this screen gazing robbing us of something inherently more valuable?

Around the same time as the conference, Pope Tawadros II, head of the Coptic Orthodox Church in Egypt, decided to shut down his official Facebook page. He explained,

Pope of Alexandria & Patriarch of All Africa on the Holy Apostolic See of Saint Mark the Evangelist of the Coptic Orthodox Church of Alexandria

> *Time is the most precious gift God gives us daily, and we must use it in a good way. The Christian must sanctify his time, and the monk leaves everything behind so that all of life becomes sanctified for God.*[1]

Pope Tawadros discovered that technology was beginning to control and restrict his prayer life. Fortunately, he remembered an ancient idea that caused him to change his behavior: the sanctification of time.

To sanctify means to make holy. Because time is part of God's creation, ordering time is a way of honoring what God has created and blessed. Monks have a duty to respect the gift of time and use it wisely. That is true for all of us.

In her book, *The Extinction of Experience*, Christine Rosen recounts the experience of visiting the Abbey of Gethsemani, once the home of writer and Trappist monk Thomas Merton. She followed the daily routine of the monastery, which begins withVigils at 3:15 am, followed by Lauds at 5:45 am, and throughout the day the offices Terce, Sext, None, and Vespers, ending with Compline at 7:30 pm. She discovered that living according to the times of the offices "fosters a completely different experience of time."[2]

Rosen experienced time at the monastery in terms of *waiting*. In the reciting of Scripture and in the common prayers, the community enters a time ordered and dedicated to God. She noted that the monks

> *...are not merely waiting to hear the voice of God. They are joyfully anticipating it, and so their wait isn't painful but pleasurable.*[3]

Perhaps the best example of the sanctification of time is the Eucharist. Jesus is present to us in the meal he shared with his disciples. The theologian Fr. Gerard Loughlin explains,

> *The Christian Eucharist remains...as the site where time continues to arrive from past and future, constituting the present moment through the church's recollection and anticipation of what is promised: the ever-renewed arrival of God's eternity in Christ...The Eucharistic celebration teaches the church how to wait upon the arrival of God.*[4]

The ritual act of remembrance comprises part of our waiting. In particular, Christians remember the story of salvation through its events, such as the Passover or the Resurrection. This means that worship is not simply a pious re-enactment of a past event, but a dynamic ordering of time through the remembrance of God's intervention in history.

This experience of God's time in worship and ritual unites us with God and places us within the frame of God's story. But how do we sanctify time outside of regular attendance at Church? For a more holistic approach, we can learn from the Celtic tradition. Esther de Waal describes:

> *A people who farmed and knew the patterns of the seasons, who lived close to the sea and watched the ebb and flow of tides, above all who watched the daily cycle of the sun and the changing path of the moon, brought all of this into their prayer...I am reminded that as a human being living on this earth, I am part of the pattern of day and night, darkness and light, the waxing and waning of the moon, and the rising and setting of the sun. The whole of myself is inserted into the rhythm of the elements and I can here learn something, if I am prepared to, of the ebb and flow of time and of life itself.*[5]

The natural world enfolds humanity into its cycles and rhythms. These cycles influence the ordering of human time, and the monastic ordering of the day is an example of how time can be sanctified within the "ebb and flow" of the natural world. The rhythms of days beginning and ending become natural metaphors for journeys undertaken, of the divine encountered, and destinations reached.

Am I saying we need to use our time more purposefully? In a way, yes, provided it includes the pastime of daydreaming. Part of the sanctification of time involves dreaming about the world, ourselves, and our relationship to God. The bridge between time and eternity is the dream. Jesus has entered time and lays claim to our subconscious mind. Daydreaming helps us to know God and experience moments of transcendence, where time stands still, and God is present among us.

St. Augustine speaks of God as "beauty ever ancient, ever new," and the Book of Revelation describes God as one "who is and who was and who is to come" (Revelation 1:8). Identifying ourselves within time and outside of time—in eternity—is the fruit of the sanctification of time. In doing so, we are turning away from ourselves and toward God.

From flip phones to Facebook, careful consideration of how we spend our time will be of benefit to us, especially those who spend large amounts of their time online. In the modern world, the internet may be the greatest thief of time. Pope Tawadros II saw a danger in the overuse of technology, becoming aware of its addictive nature. His solution was to remove himself from Facebook. When Christine Rosen visited the Abbey of Gethsemani, the abbot counseled her to "make time every day for silence". What would she do in that time? He told her, "Don't make it a chore. Just sit in silence. This allows you to listen to God".[6]

What sets humanity apart from the rest of creation is our capacity for reflection. Using our time wisely honors and blesses God. In practice, it means stepping away from those things which distract or divert us from God. In his letter to the Ephesians, St. Paul counsels, "Be careful then how you live, not as unwise people but as wise, making the most of the time." (Ephesians 5:15-16)

Most people are aware of the passing of time, but there is a saying, "There is no time like the present." It may not be possible to stop time, but you can close this book now and offer the next fifteen minutes to God. As you do, ask God to sanctify the time. Take a deep breath, then breathe out and listen for God's voice.

Notes

1.   Pope Tawadros II, August 5, 2018,
<https://www.newsofbahrain.com/world/45986.html.>

Accessed, December 11, 2024.

2.   Christine Rosen, *The Extinction of Experience* (New York: Norton, 2024) 100.

3.   Rosen, *The Extinction of Experience*, 101.

4.   Gerard Loughlin, *Telling God's Story* (Cambridge: CUP, 1996), 232.

5.   Esther de Waal, *The Celtic Way of Prayer* (New York: Doubleday, 1997) 61-62

6.   Rosen, *The Extinction of Experience*, 101.

Chapter 23

The Narrowing

Last week, I had a dream of water flowing over a rock. That was the entire dream. Unlike previous dreams, there were no people from the past or bizarre happenings or byzantine plots—only a simple scene of flowing water. In truth, a less interesting dream would be hard to imagine. The only distinctive part was that I was looking at the water through a tube or cylinder.

The previous day my wife and I had been out walking in the woods and had stopped at a small bridge across a stream. For a while we stood on the bridge and gazed down at the water gently flowing over the rocks below. I guess it was this tranquil scene which became the subject of my dream. It was a forgettable kind of dream, except that in my waking hours the memory of the dream keep returning. Usually my dreams evaporate like water on a hot skillet. Not this time. And why was I looking through a cylinder? (Which may or may not have been a telescope).

Dreams used to play a much larger part in my life than they do now. In fact, there was a period soon after ordination to the priesthood when dreams were instrumental in helping me sort out my life and relationships. Every time I woke after dreaming, I would write down what had happened in as much detail as possible. Over the following days, I would read and reread what I had written. Gradually, like a photograph developing in a darkroom, the meaning of the dream would be revealed.

Dreams appear throughout scripture. Jacob had a dream of a ladder reaching to heaven, with angels ascending and descending on it. (Genesis 28:11-19) Joseph and Daniel were dreamers and also interpreters of dreams. Another Joseph, the husband of Mary, was warned in a dream to flee to Egypt, to escape Herod's soldiers who wanted to kill Jesus. (Matthew 2:13).

My dream was less dramatic and actually rather boring. What did it have to say to me? The clue is that my vision was narrowed down to this one image. Without the framing device of the circle, I could have seen the entire landscape, with its trees, leaves, and birds. Instead, I was looking at one small part of it.

The narrowing of my vision allowed me to concentrate on the image of the flowing stream, which was beautiful and calming. I interpreted the gentle flow of water as indicating the ongoing love of God at a time when changes were imminent in my life and career.

Water also signifies emotion, which often accompanies change. The rock could stand for many things—it was immovable, which could be a good thing or else signify an intractable problem. Dreams usually come with a mood or feeling, and in this case, the feeling was peaceful.

If I consider this dream from a biblical point of view, I am reminded of the beautiful opening verses of Psalm 42,

> *As a deer longs for flowing streams, so my soul longs for you, O God.*
> *My soul thirsts for God, for the living God.*
> *When shall I come and behold the face of God?*

Was the dream directing me to deepen my relationship with God? It raised a question about the way I love God. In the past, I had gone down the path of mysticism and had experienced intense episodes of deep affection from and toward God. That in turn had led to ordained ministry. In the life of a working priest, there are pastoral and practical challenges that need to be addressed, often leaving less time for attending to the inner spiritual life. Was I on a circular path leading back to a deeper kind of prayer?

In the short term, the dream had one definite outcome: it led me to pray. First, to give thanks for the dream. Second, to renew my trust in God's providence for me. Finally, the dream taught me to be specific in my praying. At times I need to practice a kind of narrowing in prayer, a zeroing in on one particular subject. While God cares for all humanity and the whole of creation, at the same time he is focused on the singular and the specific.

Chapter 24

What God Requires

There would be no global Christianity were it not for those first apostles who ventured forth beyond the region of Palestine to spread the good news of Jesus Christ. Christianity was never meant to be a localized religion or cult but a movement that would sweep across the whole world. Jesus had trained the disciples for this special mission, which would depend on equal measures of courage and faith.

The history of the growth of the early church is written in the Acts of the Apostles and in the letters in the New Testament. One of the most important apostles was St. Paul. Through his evangelism and his writings, Paul had a significant influence on the theology and spread of early Christianity.

Paul was an accomplished orator and a tireless advocate for Christ. His background as a Pharisee made him eminently suitable for this work. Equipped with knowledge of the law and convinced of the immeasurable value of knowing Christ, Paul throws himself into the role of evangelist. Paul is tough, intelligent, and determined to prevail even when, on one occasion, he is shipwrecked.

His letters provide an illuminating glimpse into the challenges facing this new movement. The apostle is anxious for Christians not to fall into error and stray from the right path. Within the early churches there are divisions that Paul exhorts them to address. Paul is also working out a theology for them, which will underpin the way they will live and practice their faith.

Valentin de Boulogne (o Nicolas Tournier), Saint Paul Writing His Epistles, c. 1618 - 1620, oil on canvas, 39 1/8 × 52 3/8 in. (99.4 x 133 cm, Museum of Fine Arts, Houston, Texas.

Paul's zeal as the Lord's servant only flagged towards the end of his life, when he faced the choice between continuing to serve God, or dying and being with Jesus. In writing to the church in the city of Philippi, Paul says, "I am hard pressed between the two: my desire is to depart and be with Christ, for that is far better, but to remain in the flesh is more necessary." (Philippians 1:23)

This is not really a dilemma for Paul In fact, he is describing what are, in effect, two sides of the same coin. So ardent is his love and desire for Christ, that Paul simply longs for death, knowing that Christ will welcome him into heaven. On the other hand, Paul knows that he has been specially chosen by Christ who calls him to the world, to a life dedicated to teaching the gospel and establishing new churches.

In Paul's letters we discover a faithful disciple of Jesus who searches for the answer to this basic question, "What does it mean to be a Christian?" Although he is able to expound on this subject at great length, he always reaches the same conclusion: to be a Christian means to be "in Christ." As he writes to the church in Galatia, "…it is no longer I who live, but it is Christ who lives in me." (Galatians 2:20)

A close identification with Christ means more than agreeing with Christ's teachings. Christians do not follow a set of statements about life. In Paul's view, Christians follow Christ who is the Savior of the world. Christian wisdom is therefore predicated on the revelation of God in Jesus Christ. Since Christ's teachings are founded in love, we can only understand fully the power of Christ's love through loving Christ ourselves.

Of course, love creates a desire to be with the object of one's love; hence Paul's desire to be with Christ in heaven. Yet Paul is wise enough to know that love's desire can be directed in other ways, which is why he mentions his own role as evangelist and facilitator of the new Christian churches. And while Paul commits himself to undertake this work as a servant and lover of Christ, something else is happening: Paul himself is being transformed by his own self-offering.

It's natural to take a human-centered approach to understanding Paul. But what if one were to take a God-centered view of Paul? Why does God require Paul to keep working rather than fulfill his heart's desire and call him home? The obvious answer is that God had a need for Paul, and it is hard to imagine early Christianity—especially its theology—without Paul's colossal and valuable contribution.

I recalled Paul's words when I was counseling two members of the church who happened to be presented with similar experiences. It seemed an unusual coincidence that both came to me within a two-week period. Their own situations were different, but there were fundamental similarities to their stories which chimed and echoed what Paul had been describing in his letters. Both were asking themselves the question: "What does God require of me?"

Their stories are obviously personal and I have sought their permission to relate them here. Both have seen this meditation and are happy for their stories to be publicly known (although they remain anonymous).

The first member had been suicidal and had sought relief through drink. One evening she had drunk herself to sleep and then dreamed that she had gone to heaven. On her arrival, she was greeted by her father's friend, a

Methodist minister, who had died some years ago. He explained that, although she was troubled, it would be best if she were to resolve her issues while living. She then awoke with a new resolve to live.

The second member started our conversation by expressing her love for Jesus. I told her that God needed lovers but alas, there were too few. Then she said that Jesus was prompting her to address an unresolved issue in her own life.

It turned out that the unresolved issues for both women centered on family members who were dying. In the first case, there had been a recent family argument that had been traumatic; on the face of it, the break seemed irreparable. In the second case, the member had not spoken to her brother for over twenty years. Now that he was dying she felt compelled to see him one last time.

"What does God require?" Their Christian faith had kindled in them the need for reconciliation. It only remained for them to discern how to make it a reality.

Both members were wishing to follow Christ's teachings in their lives. As we look towards heaven, God is reminding us to attend to the things of earth. Since the gospel message is personal, it is in the realm of relationships that our calling as Christians is being directed. The mature Christian gradually learns to release their self-centered view of themselves and of their relationships and learns to adopt God's point of view.

A sad example of the self-centered view was presented to me a number of years ago. A man attending a friend's baptism told me that, because he was "saved", there was nothing further he needed to do. He didn't come to church regularly because, logically, there was no need. I felt sorry for him because it seemed as though he had been converted on an instant ticket to heaven, which saved him the trouble of having to make any effort to get there. This kind of dangerous thinking takes root when the consequences of salvation are not properly explained, or when churches are so desperate for converts that they mislead them into thinking that grace can be obtained cheaply.

The solution is to adopt God's point of view. "What does God require of me?" The two members who came to me had the good sense to persevere in a relationship with Jesus. Through the love of Jesus, God had revealed to them what God required. In each case, there were broken relationships in need of repair. As one of them said, "God told me, 'Don't wait until you get to heaven before you resolve this problem. I want you to deal with it before you get here.'"

For the two members who came to me for counseling, God revealed that the gospel was like a half-finished sentence written on their hearts, where the completing part of the sentence was on their lips. In trust and humility, they took on the challenge of resolving their problems and repairing the broken parts of their lives. At first, there was pain and then healing and then peace. The Lord God blessed them because of their willingness to listen to God and act accordingly.

St. Paul also listened to God. From Jesus, he received the assurance of peace and companionship in the life to come. He counted himself among the laborers in the vineyard who toiled to plant, sow, and reap, often in the face of hostility and hardship. Faith and determination bore him onward until the time came for the work to pass to another, and Paul at last joined his beloved Jesus in heaven.

Psalm 42

Behind the Church of the Messiah in Lower Gwynedd there is a large graveyard that provides a resting place for many of our former members. As I look out my office window, I occasionally see deer wandering through the yard. These magnificent creatures appear unexpectedly and vanish just as quickly. I have an unfulfilled wish that, while they are touring the graveyard, they will eat the weeds along the gravel paths. And yes, I know that deer are a pest, but whenever I see them my heart is lifted.

My affection for these stately animals derives, in part, from the reference to them in Psalm 42, which begins, "As a deer longs for flowing streams, so my soul longs for you, O God." The psalmist is writing on behalf of those who love God with an ardent passion. Water is a symbol of life, and the deer is a symbol of the soul which longs for God. The psalmist is one who does not wait for God to come to them, but searches for God as the deer searches for water, in order that he or she may live.

Psalm 42 has another memorable line: "Deep calls to deep at the thunder of your cataracts; all your waves and your billows have gone over me." This verse can be understood as referring to the overwhelming love of God which, like a torrent of water, is far deeper and stronger than we can control or manage.

However, another interpretation of these lines is possible: it could be a description of someone drowning. This latter meaning was brought home to me during a meeting of pilgrims who had recently visited the Holy Land. As each pilgrim recalled one event that was special for them, one of them said "You don't really know Christ until you are drowning."

Many have found Jesus to be a savior in times of crisis. Jesus is present at all times in our lives, as the next line of the psalm affirms, "By day the Lord commands his steadfast love, and at night his song is with me, a prayer to the God of my life."

The psalmist describes both the peace and tumult of a relationship with God. However, the tumult is not to be found in God, but in ourselves. The faithfulness and steadfastness of God's love is what keeps the fearful and disturbed soul from drowning, since God is never absent, even when we begin to sink beneath the waves of sorrow and oppression.

The final verse of the psalm sums up the situation of the writer, "Why are you cast down, O my soul, and why are you disquieted within me? Hope in God; for I shall again praise him, my help and my God." Hard times can be a test of our faith. People of faith don't always have an easy time, but the psalmist reminds us that God is always with us and that we can call upon him any time of the day or night.

Chapter 26

Zone Of Totality

Zone of Totality is a movie which premieres in 2035. Based on the science fiction novella of the same name, it describes what happens when the moon is knocked off its orbit after being struck by a giant asteroid. Every day thereafter, the moon blocks the sun's rays for exactly three minutes and forty-nine seconds.

The "zone" includes the area around Lower Gwynedd, North Wales, and Lansdale, Pennsylvania. At 3:00 pm every day, the sky grows dark and people stop what they are doing. Instead of the golden light of late afternoon, the landscape is bathed in a platinum light. Neighbors, family, and friends gather together to witness this unexpected wonder, their voices a mixture of murmuring and laughter.

As the plot unfolds, Church leaders designate the area as a religious zone of interest. "God has spoken to us", declared the presiding bishop of the Episcopal Church. "Henceforth, every day at 3:00 pm, we will offer our praise and thanksgiving for what God has done. Let prayer be your response. May the Lord be in your mind, on your lips, and in your heart."

The collective and daily utterance of prayer became routine in the lives of the population. Some believers from out of state even sold their homes and went to live in the "zone", so that they could participate fully in the daily ritual. People brought their sick and troubled, and many were healed by the fervent prayers of the people. Daily arguments were deferred until the "Zone of Totality" began, with disputes being resolved under the platinum light of prayer.

The population grew and expanded beyond the area of Lower Gwynedd, North Wales, and Lansdale. Eventually, the people discovered something remarkable: it became possible to step outside of the "zone" and still enjoy the benefits of it. People everywhere gathered daily in prayer for three

Church of the Messiah, Lower Gwynedd, Pennsylvania.

minutes and forty-nine seconds. The soul of the country was transformed and revitalized by this simple observance. In gratitude, some made an annual pilgrimage to the Zone of Totality and kept the memory of that visit close to their hearts.

Sadly, it all came to an end when, one day, the moon was struck for a second time by an asteroid, and resumed its previous orbit. The daily eclipse was over.

An old timer told his grandchildren the story of the Zone of Totality. "For a short time", he reminisced, "the whole country came together to experience healing and a common purpose. We all felt blessed by God."

The movie ends in the churchyard of the Church of the Messiah, Lower Gwynedd. Sunlight dances on the graves of the departed as light falls through the trees. Along the line of headstones walks a solitary figure. After a while she stops by a large dial made of white marble, set in the ground. There are fresh flowers next to the dial. Placing her hands together, she offers a quiet prayer. She closes her eyes and feels the shifting patterns of sunlight on her face. It is a moment of understanding—of re-awakening—both for her and for the audience.

Bibliography

Amis, Martin, *Koba the Dread*, (New York: Hyperion Press, 2002)

Butler, John, *The Red Dean* (London: Scala Publishers, 2011)

Chidester, David, *Christianity* (London: Allen Lane, 2000)

Conquest, Robert, *Reflections on a Ravaged Century*, (New York: W.W. Norton & Co., 2000)

Del Noce, Augusto, *The Problem of Atheism*, edited and translated by Carlo Lancellotti, (Montreal: McGill-Queens University Press, 2021)

de Waal, Esther, *The Celtic Way of Prayer* (New York: Doubleday, 1997)

Dreyer, Rod, "Pope's 'Common Dreams' With Marxists Denies Persecution Nightmare" *The European Conservative*, January 11, 2024. <https://europeanconservative.com/articles/Commentary/popes-marxist-dreams/> {accessed January 20, 2024}

Engels Frederick, "The Condition of England: A Review of Past and Present", by Thomas Carlyle, London 1843. (January 1844), *Deutsch-Französische Jahrbücher*, 1844. In: *Marx/Engels Selected Works*, Volume 3 (Progress Publishers, 1970)

Goldman, Emma, *My Two Years in Russia* (St Petersburg: Red and Black, 2008)

Guiver, George, *All Christians Are Monks*, (Durham: Sacristy Press, 2024)

Hilarion, Metropolitan, *Theology of Icon in the Orthodox Church*, Lecture at St. Vladimir's Seminary, 5 February 2011. <https://mospat.ru/en/news/56024/> Accessed December 9, 2024

Horowitz, David, *Radical Son (30th Anniversary Edition)* (New York: Bombadier Books, 2020)

Huxley, Aldous, "Introduction" to *Erewhon*, by Samuel Butler. (New York: Limited Editions Club, 1934) Koestler, Arthur, "The Initiates" in *The God That Failed*, ed. Richard Crossman (London: Hamilton,1950)

Lewis, C. S., *Mere Christianity* (London: Harper Collins, expanded edition 2001)

Loughlin, Gerard, *Telling God's Story* (Cambridge: CUP, 1996)

Maier, Frances X. , "How Marxism Won the war of Ideas", *Wall Street Journal*, January 6, 2022. <https://www.wsj.com/articles/marxism-won-war-of-ideas-augusto-del-noce-gnosticism-catholic-therapy-ai-mental-health-technology-11641483920> [accessed February 14, 2022]

McMeekin, Sean, *To Overthrow the World* (NewYork: Basic Books, 2024)

Norman, Edward, *Christianity and the World Order* (Oxford: OUP, 1979)

Nouwen, Henri, "Adam's Place" in *Shadow and Light*, Eds. Darryl Tippens, Stephen Weathers, Jack Welch (Abilene: A.C.U. Press, 1997)

Ouspensky, Leonid and Lossky, Vladimir, *The Meaning of Icons* (Olten: Otto Walter, 1952)

Peris, Daniel, *Storming the Heavens* (New York: Cornell University Press, 1998)

Pope Tawadros II, August 5, 2018, <https://www.newsofbahrain.com/world/45986.html.> Accessed, December 11, 2024

Pryce-Jones David, "Eric Hobsbawm:Lying to the Credulous" in *Openings and Outings* (New York: Criterion, 2022)

"Richard Dawkins attacks 'irrelevant' religion in Rowan Williams debate", *Daily Telegraph*, February 1, 2013. <https://www.telegraph.co.uk/news/religion/9841063/Richard-Dawkins-attacks-irrelevant-religion-in-Rowan-Williams-debate.html#:~:text=In his address, Lord Williams,dare I say it, inclusion> [accessed December 6, 2024]

Rogers, Benedict, "Why China is Terrified of Christianity" *Unherd*, February 17, 2021. <https:// unherd.com/2021/02/why-china-is-terrified-of-christianity/> {accessed February 14, 2022)

Rosen, Christine, *The Extinction of Experience* (New York: Norton, 2024)

Smolkin, Victoria, *A Sacred Space is Never Empty* (Princeton: Princeton University Press, 2018)

Spender, Stephen, "Worshipers From Afar" in *The God That Failed*, ed. Richard Crossman (London: Hamilton, 1950)

Stern, Ludmila, *Western Intellectuals and the Soviet Union 1920-40* (Abingdon: Routledge, 2007)

St. John Damascene, *On Holy Images* (London: Thomas Baker, 1898)

St. Theodore the Studite, *On the Holy Icons* (New York: SVS Press, 1997)

Williams, Rowan, *The Poems of Rowan Williams*, (Oxford:Perpetua Press, 2002)

Zelensky, Elizabeth and Gilbert, Lela, *Windows to Heaven* (Grand Rapids: Brazos Press, 2005)

About the Author

David Beresford currently serves as Interim Associate Rector at Christ Church Christiana Hundred in the Episcopal Diocese of Delaware. Ordained in the Church of England, he served in the Dioceses of Chichester and St. Albans before emigrating to the USA in 2016. He has designed and led Adult Formation courses on *Faith and Poetry*, *Knowing God* and *Word Into Life*, and writes a weekly meditation on his website https:// davidberesford.net. He is the author of *Above & Below* and *Call to Love*. He lives in Wilmington, Delaware with his wife Ruth, and their cat Mani.

Colophon

Blessed by God was designed in Italy by Bob Schwartz on an Apple MacPro using Adobe InDesign and Photoshop CC. The book's title is set in forty-seven-point Amadine. Chapter titles are set in twenty-four-point Ginger. The primary text is set in twelve-point Perpetua, fourteen-point leaded. The front and back material titles are set in fourteen-point Avenir, and the text is set in ten-point Avenir, thirteen-point leaded.

Amandine is a modern high-contrast sans serif typeface designed by the Russian-born type designer Elena Genova of the My Creative Land foundry in Edinburgh, United Kingdom. Amandine's design is inspired by forms from the Didone font family, with some influence from vintage typefaces and calligraphy scripts.

Ginger is a sleek, geometric sans-serif font inspired by the typefaces of Paul Renner and Herb Lubalin. The typeface was designed by Rick Banks, Shaqa Bovand, and Ryan Williamson and released by the F37 Foundry of Manchester, United Kingdom in 2013.

Designed by the English sculptor and stonemason Eric Gill, Perpetua is a crisp, contemporary serif typeface that does not follow any particular historical model. Perpetua's design was commissioned by Stanley Morison, an influential historian of printing and adviser to the Monotype Foundry, in 1925— a time when Gill's reputation as an artist-craftsman was high. Perpetua, which is particularly popular in fine book printing, is named for the Christian martyr Vibia Perpetua.

Avenir is a geometric sans-serif typeface designed by Adrian Ftutiger and released by Linotype GmbH in 1988. The word avenir is French for future, and the family takes inspiration from the geometric style of sans-serif typefaces developed in the 1920s—such as Erbar and Futura—that used the circle as the basis for their design.

www.ingramcontent.com/pod-product-compliance
Lightning Source LLC
Chambersburg PA
CBHW040802090726
47818CB00068B/241